ANCESTOR-WORSHIP AND JAPANESE LAW

Eschewing the path of religious pamphleteering in favour of a broad juridical and sociological approach, Professor Hozumi describes the practice of Japanese Ancestor-worship, its origins, manifestations, peculiarities and social and legal implications. The author lays aside many misconceptions regarding Ancestor-worship, permitting us to see Japanese cultures and religions in an entirely new light. Among the fascinating topics covered are Ancestor-worship in Europe and America, the theory of the dread of ghosts, sacred places in the Japanese house, and the relation of Ancestor-worship to loyalty and patriotism.

THE AUTHOR IN HIS FORTY-SIXTH YEAR (1900)

ANCESTOR-WORSHIP AND JAPANESE LAW

BARON NOBUSHIGE HOZUMI

LONDON AND NEW YORK

Originally published in 1940 by Hokuseido
First published in 2004 by Kegan Paul.

This edition first published in 2009 by
Routledge
2 Park Square, Milton Park, Abingdon, Oxfordshire OX14 4RN

Simultaneously published in the USA and Canada
by Routledge
711 Third Avenue, New York, NY 10017

First issued in paperback 2016

Routledge is an imprint of the Taylor & Francis Group, an informa business

© Kegan Paul, 2004

All rights reserved. No part of this book may be reprinted or reproduced or utilised in any form or by any electronic, mechanical, or other means, now known or hereafter invented, including photocopying and recording, or in any information storage or retrieval system, without permission in writing from the publishers.

British Library Cataloguing in Publication Data
A catalogue record for this book is available from the British Library

ISBN 13: 978-1-138-96667-3 (pbk)
ISBN 13: 978-0-7103-1000-2 (hbk)

Publisher's Note
The publisher has gone to great lengths to ensure the quality of this reprint but points out that some imperfections in the original copies may be apparent. The publisher has made every effort to contact original copyright holders and would welcome correspondence from those they have been unable to trace.

PREFACE

The present volume is based upon an address delivered by me at the International Congress of Orientalists held at Rome in October 1899. The object of the original lecture was to show the close relation which exists between Ancestor-worship and Japanese Law, and the vast influence which the former exercised upon different branches of the latter. It was, therefore, intended to be a juridical as well as a sociological study, and not meant to be a religious tract. For that reason, I was careful not to trespass upon religious or theological grounds; and however interesting or enticing might be the discussion of such questions as "Whether Ancestor-worship was the root of all religions," or such subjects as the "Relation of Ancestor-worship and Christianity in Japan," I was obliged to resist the strong temptation, and keep myself strictly within the bounds of my original plan. There was, therefore, not a word in the first edition of this work, which might be taken as depreciating Christianity, or praising Ancestor-worship at the expense of other forms of worship.

I was, in consequence, not a little surprised to find some criticisms of this book coming from the pens of Christian missionaries, severely attacking the practice of Ancestor-worship and my book, which they evidently took for advocating Ancestor-worship at the expense of Christianity. Perhaps my statement that the introduction of Western civilization into this country did not shake the wide-spread and persistent faith of the people, was too sweeping to win the cordial assent of some of the enthusiastic teachers of Christianity, who may have taken it as a slight upon the success of their work. One of them wrote in a language, which one does not usually expect from those quarters. An extract will show the general tone of his argument. Referring probably to the words "it may perhaps be of some interest to examine the subject from within, and discuss it from the point of view of an ancestor-worshipper himself," he wrote:—"this popular professor, while he loves most heartily the tradition of his country, is carried too far by his own devotion to ancestor-worship, of which he is astonishingly proud." Far be it from me to be guilty of a vice, which I most detest! If the simple confession of being an ancestor-worshipper conveys any idea of pride, I have only to be ashamed of my ignorance of the English language.

But this was only one of the many offences, of which I was guilty. I was accused, among others, of completely ignoring the result of modern historical criticism by mentioning Amaterasu Ō-Mikami as the First Imperial Ancestor. The critic concludes "'Man is made in the image of God.' Men everywhere are of divine descent. Their First Ancestor is the One Living Creator and Father of all men.... And what can be better for Japan and every Japanese family, nay, for all the families of the whole world, than to join in the sincere worship of the God and Father of all our loved ancestors?" The critic's statement is no doubt borne out by "modern historical criticism." Be that as it may, I am glad to learn from him that Christians are ancestor-worshippers after all.

However, I did not feel called upon at that time to reply to those criticisms, not only because they were beyond the scope of my book, but also because I had a high respect for the personal character of the writers. However interesting and important—especially to the missionaries—the calm examination of the question whether the practice of Ancestor-worship is incompatible with the doctrine of Christianity—whether the manifestation, in a certain manner, of the feeling of love and respect towards one's ancestors is against the First Commandment, and not in accordance with the Fifth Commandment—or in other words, whether a good ancestor-worshipper can not be at the same time a good Christian, the scope of my work and lack of time obliged me to suppress the strong inducement to make a reply and discuss that question with them. So, I turned to them the other cheek, like a good Christian, and felt all the better for it.

Moreover, the recent appearance of the late Lafcadio Hearn's "Japan," of Professor Y. Haga's "The Ten Treatises on the National Character" (國民性十論), and of Professor J. Takakusu's "The Basis of the National Morality" (國民道德の根抵) happily relieves me of involving myself in a religious controversy, which is extremely distasteful to me. Most of what I might have said in reply are said in those works, so that I have only to refer to them here, and content myself with citing a few passages from them.

The late Lafcadio Hearn's book is full of warnings—and what I take to be kind advices—to Christian zealots in the Far East, and he concludes it thus :—" Never will the East turn Christian while dogmatism requires the convert to deny his ancient obligation to the family, the community, and the government,—and further insists that he prove his zeal for an alien creed by destroying the tablets of his ancestors, and outraging the memory of those who gave him life." He attributes what he calls " smallness of results of modern missions " in the East to the needless and implacable attacks upon ancestor-cult, and goes on to say :—" To demand of a Chinese or an Annamese that he cast away or destroy his ancestral tablets is not less irrational and inhuman than it would be to demand of an Englishman or a Frenchman that he destroy his mother's tombstone in proof of his devotion to Christianity."

Professor Haga's book " The Ten Treatises on the National Character," which was published some years after the first edition of this work appeared, contains a very interesting article on Ancestor-worship. After explaining that the success of the Buddhists in propagating their religion in Japan was due chiefly to their wise reconciliation with the national practice, he goes on :—" But the newly introduced Christian religion now and then comes into conflict with the people on this point. Christians do not have *Kami-dana* in the house. Saying that they would not bow before anybody but God, they sometimes refuse to do homage to the portrait of the Emperor, or dislike visiting the Great Shrine of the First Imperial Ancestor. This comes probably from their ignorance of the fundamental character of our Empire, and their confounding the reverence for the Imperial Ancestral Mausoleum with religion. Nobody is justified in refusing to bow before his parents ! " The same professor, after stating that the Minatogawa Shrine, dedicated to the loyal Kusunoki Masashige, the Taiwan Shrine, dedicated to the late Imperial Prince Kita-Shirakawa, who died in Formosa during the war with China, the Yasukuni Shrine, dedicated to all persons who died for the country, and other such shrines, are all established for the worship of our forefathers, who had done meritorious service to the State, and that it is quite a proper thing that subsequent generations should show gratitude and do homage to the memory of those great personages, says :—" The believers of the foreign religion seem to dislike even this. But where is the difference between this and our saluting Admiral Tōgō, recognizing his great exploit? In Western countries, we see everywhere stone or bronze statues of great men, which not only serve as ornaments of towns, but are also made objects of veneration. In Germany, for instance, we see the statues of William the Great, or of Prince Bismarck erected in almost all towns throughout the country, and the people pay respect to the memories of those great men on their anniversaries by offering wreaths to the statues. This comes from man's natural sentiment, and the shrines in our country come from no other source. All the difference, if any, comes to this,—that they erect statues and we establish shrines. To say that it is right to pay respect to the bronze statues, but wrong to visit and do homage to the shrines is a contradiction in itself. No one will be justified in saying that, while it is perfectly proper to visit the graves of one's relatives and friends, it is below one's dignity or against one's religious faith to do homage to the shrines of great men. All these inconsistencies come from their misunderstanding of the word 'kami,' and confusing the worship of shrines with religion."

I look with sincere regret upon frequent conflicts that arise between the missionaries or newly-converted Christians and our people who are ancestor-worshippers; for I am one of those who firmly believe that the practice of Ancestor-worship is not incompatible with Christianity. It is not contrary to the First Commandment, because the ancestral spirit is nothing more than the outcome of the belief in the immortality of soul, and can not be considered as " gods," which the "jealous God" forbids to worship. If Ancestor-worship is, as maintained in this book, the extension of love and respect to distant forefathers, the manifestation of the love and respect in a certain harmless way may be regarded as a realization of the Fifth Commandment to honour the parents; and nothing against Christianity, which is essentially a religion of love.

Offering of food, drink or flowers, bowing before ancestral tablets, or visiting ancestral graves are very often regarded as superstitious practices; and I do not deny it. But, where is a religion which is entirely free from superstition? Every religion—Christianity included—has more or less of rituals which may be characterized as superstitions. Only the most advanced religions have the least amount of them. Christianity—especially its Protestant sect—is certainly one of them, and Ancestor-worship—if it is regarded as a religion—is another. What remains of superstitious formalisms or rituals among civilized people are only those which are harmless or natural. If Ancestor-worship is regarded as a manifestation of love and respect towards distant kinsmen, it may also be regarded as a moral practice; and it is for that reason that some among us object to the use of the word "Ancestor-worship" and propose to replace it with "Ancestor-reverence."

The expense of bringing out the present edition was borne by the Hozumi Foundation for the Encouragement of Legal Science. That Foundation was established in 1906 by my friends and pupils to commemorate my twenty-five years' service in the Tokyo Imperial University. I take this as a proper opportunity to acknowledge publicly my deep sense of gratitude towards the subscribers to the endowment of that Foundation, who numbered more than one thousand, for their kindness in thus memorializing my small share in the legal education of this country. I have also to return my hearty thanks to the directors of the Foundation, Professors

Keijirō Okano, Saburō Yamada and Kōtarō Shida for proposing to appropriate the income of the Foundation, in the first place, to the publication of my book, and to the members of the Council for unanimously resolving to adopt the proposal and make it the first act of the Foundation.

The lecture was published in its original form in 1901, and in the same year a German translation by Dr. Paul Brunn appeared. More than a decade has elapsed since the first issue, and in the meantime many important events have happened, such as the war with Russia and the publication of many important Imperial House Ordinances, which made it necessary or advisable that I should make alterations and corrections in many places. Accordingly, I have thoroughly revised the original lecture, reconsidered and rewritten it, and made considerable additions to it, so that the present issue can scarcely be called a second edition.

In issuing this edition, I have considered many

PREFACE xvii

kind suggestions and valuable criticisms, with which I was favoured, and I have taken full advantage of them. To the many persons who have in this or other ways assisted me in my work I tender my hearty thanks. First of all, to my friend Mr. Kazutomo Takahashi, chief editor of the Japan Times, who kindly read over the manuscript of this edition and gave me many suggestions as to corrections and improvements, which were most valuable to me. To Dr. S. R. Steinmetz, a great authority on ethnology, who kindly gave me valuable informations, and confirmed me in my view as to the universality of the practice of Ancestor-worship among primitive peoples—a view which I stated with much diffidence in the first edition. To my friends and colleagues, Professors J. Sakurai and Y. Hijikata, the former for giving me valuable advices, the latter for pointing out all the typographical errors in the first edition. Last, but not least, to Mr. Kanesada Hanazono, my son Shigetō and my daughter-in-law Nakako, who read over the proof-sheets and otherwise assisted me in the preparation of this book for the second edition.

N. Hozumi.

Tokyo, July, 1912.

Preface to The Third Edition

In issuing the present edition, I have to express my great obligation to Baron D. Kikuchi, whose kind interest in his friend's work has shown itself in reading through the last edition of this book immediately after its publication and giving me many valuable suggestions. Besides the necessary corrections and alterations, the present edition is substantially the same as the last, except that a few illustrations have been inserted.

N. H.

CONTENTS

INTRODUCTION

	PAGE
Ancestor-worship in Europe and America	1
Ancestor-worship in Japan	1
Influence of Confucianism	2
Influence of Buddhism	2
Influence of Western civilization	2
Present state of Ancestor-worship	3

PART I

Ancestor-Worship in General

CHAPTER I

THE ORIGIN OF ANCESTOR-WORSHIP

Theory of the dread of ghosts and ghost-propitiation	7
Opinion of Lord Avebury	7
Opinion of Ihering	7
Extension of filial love	9
Treatment of the aged	10
Opinions of Chu-hsi and Kurita	12
Two kinds of ghosts	14
Lares and *larvae*	14
Confucius on filial piety	15
Henry Irving as Hamlet	16

CONTENTS

	PAGE
Opinion of Dr. E. B. Tylor	18
Love of ghosts	19

CHAPTER II

ANCESTOR-WORSHIP AS THE ORIGIN OF SOCIAL LIFE

Conscious aims of association	20
Unconscious force of association	21
Consanguinity as a bond of union	21
Extension of love and sympathy to distant kinsmen	22
Worship of the common ancestor as centripetal force	23
Whether Ancestor-worship is a universal institution among primitive peoples	24
Opinions of Tylor, Maine, Coulanges, Hearn and Steinmetz	24

PART II

Ancestor-Worship in Japan

CHAPTER I

THREE KINDS OF ANCESTOR-WORSHIP

Two sacred places in the Japanese house	30
Kamidana, or the god-shelf	30
Butsudan, or the Buddhist altar	30
Worship of the Imperial Ancestors	30
The First Imperial Ancestor	30
The Daijingū at Isé	30
Taima or *Ōnusa*	30

	PAGE
Worship of clan-ancestors	31
Uji-gami, or local tutelary god	31
Worship of family-ancestors	31
Mitamashiro	31
Ancestral tablet	32

CHAPTER II

THE WORSHIP OF THE IMPERIAL ANCESTORS

The First Imperial Ancestor	33
Three places of worship	33
Daijingū	33
Kashiko-Dokoro	33
Kamidana	33
The Divine Mirror	34
The Great Shrine at Isé	34
Pilgrimage to the Great Shrine	35
The Three Temples in the Sanctuary of the Imperial Palace	36
The Imperial House Ordinance relating to Festivals	37
Great Festivals	37
Small Festivals	43
National holidays	45

CHAPTER III

THE WORSHIP OF CLAN-ANCESTORS

Three classes of the Japanese people	47
Divine Branch, or *Shin-betsu*	47
Imperial Branch, or *Kwō-betsu*	47

	PAGE
Foreign Branch, or *Ban-betsu*	47
Clan-names, *uji* and *kabane*	47
Meanings of *uji* and *kabane*	47
Great clan, or *ō-uji*	49
Small clan, or *ko-uji*	49
Clan-god, or *uji-gami*	50
Festival of the clan-god	51
Change in the meaning of the word *uji-gami*	52
Uji-gami as an eponym	52
Uji-gami as a local patron-god	52
Uji-ko, or " children of the clan "	53

CHAPTER IV

The Worship of Family-Ancestors

Three periods of home-worship	54
Sacrifice-days, or *ki-nichi*	54
Sacrifice-months, or *shō-tsuki*	54
Sacrifice-years, or *nen-ki*	54
" Seventh-day services " among Buddhists	55
" Tenth-day services " among Shintōists	56
Shintō rituals	56
Shintō prayer, or *norito*	57
Sacredness of the ancestral name	58
Custom of " declaring name " on the battlefield	59
Examples from history	59
Example from *Nō* drama	60
Buddhist rituals	63
Three appointed times of worship	64
Higan, or the vernal equinoctial festival	64
Higan, or the autumnal equinoctial festival	65
Urabon, or the *Bon* Festival	65

CONTENTS xxiii

PAGE
Anniversary festivals of the ancestors of the Shōguns 67
Custom of visiting ancestral graves 68

PART III

Ancestor-Worship and Law

CHAPTER I

THE GOVERNMENT

Matsuri-goto, or "affairs of worship" 71
Ceremony of the "Commencement of the Affairs of the State" 71
"*Sai-sei Itchi*," or the "unity of worship and government" 72
The Department of Divine Worship 72
The Taihō Code and the Yengi Shiki 72
Report of important State affairs to the Great Shrine . 72
Visits of the Emperor and the Crown Prince to the Great Shrine 73
Visits of Prince Itō and Admiral Tōgō to the Great Shrine 73

CHAPTER II

THE CONSTITUTION

Promulgation of the Constitution 75
Prince Itō and the Imperial Commission 75
The fundamental principle of the Constitution . . . 75
Prince Itō's "Commentaries on the Constitution" . 76

CONTENTS

	PAGE
The Preamble of the Constitution	76
The Imperial Speech	77
The Imperial Oath	79
The Preamble of the Imperial House Law	81
The Supplements to the Imperial House Law	82
Imperial message to the Combined Fleet	83
The ascension of Jimmu Tennō	84
The Ceremonies of Coronation	84
Theocratico-patriarchal constitutionalism	86
Causes of this form of government	86
Insular position of Japan	86
Ancestor-worship	87
The Restoration of 1868	89
The "Five Articles of the Imperial Oath"	89

CHAPTER III

THE IMPERIAL HOUSE

The Throne as a heritage from the Imperial Ancestors	92
Imperial House Ordinances of 1909 and 1910	92
Birth	92
Naming	92
Majority	93
Marriage	94
Institution of the Imperial Heir-apparent	96
Ascension to the Throne	96
Coronation	97
Regency	98
The Imperial House Law and the Imperial House Ordinances promulgated on Kigensetsu	99
The Imperial House as "ōyaké"	100
Identification of the Imperial cult with the national cult	101

CONTENTS xxv

PAGE
Relation of Ancestor-worship to loyalty and patriotism 101
Recent revolution in China 101

CHAPTER IV

The People

"Three Bodies" 104
Uji-no-kami, or clan-chief 104
Uji as an administrative division 105
The Reform of the Taikwa Era 106
Change of administrative divisions from personal to
 territorial 106
The Imperial Rescript on Education 106
Basis of the moral education of the people 109

CHAPTER V

The House

Three epochs of the law of personal registration . . 110
  Epoch of clan-registration 110
    Kugadachi, or ordeal of hot water 111
    Bureau for the Compilation of Clan-registry . . 111
    Genealogical records 112
    The Shōji Roku 112
    Bureau of Genealogical Investigation 112
  Epoch of house-registration 113
    The Reform of the Taikwa Era 113
  Epoch of status-registration 113
    The Law of 1898 113
Clan as the original unit of the State 114
  Disintegration of the clan 114

CONTENTS

	PAGE
House as the intermediate unit of the State	114
Disintegration of the house	115
Individual as the final unit of the State	116
Provisions of the new Civil Code	116
Prohibition of the abolition of a house	117
Duty of an heir to continue the house	118
The Peerage Ordinance of 1907	119
House-laws of the Peers	119
House-law of a certain Count	120

CHAPTER VI

MARRIAGE

Definition of marriage in the Li Chi	124
Original cause of its recognition by law	124
Continuity of family cult	124
Mencius on filial impiety	125
Confucius on filial impiety	125
Consent of the house-head	126
Consent of the parents	127
Mencius on the marriage of the Emperor Shun	130
Chinese prohibition of marriage between persons of the same clan-name	130
Celibacy	131
The "Hundred Articles" of Tokugawa	131
Celibacy of younger sons	132
Concubinage	133
Cause of its legal recognition	135
Concubine's status	136
Abolition of concubinage	137

CHAPTER VII

Divorce

	PAGE
The House-law of the Taihō Code	138
" Seven grounds of divorce "	138
Sterility	139
Adultery	139
Bad disease	140
Provisions of the new Civil Code	140
Two kinds of divorce	140
Judicial divorce	140
Consensual divorce	140
Grounds of judicial divorce	140
Dissolution of adoption and divorce	141
Muko-yōshi, or " adoption of a son-in-law "	141
Kajo, or " house-daughter "	141
Daijo, or " stock-daughter "	142

CHAPTER VIII

Adoption

Object of adoption	144
Fustel de Coulanges on adoption	144
Duty of the house-head to adopt	144
Qualification of the adopter	144
Age	144
Childlessness	145
Failure of male issue	145
Consolation for childless marriage	145
" Death-bed adoption "	146
" Quick adoption "	146

CONTENTS

	PAGE
"Sudden adoption"	146
Death without an heir	147
Adoption by testament	147
Lower limit of the age of the adopter	148
The Taihō Code	148
The Tokugawa Shōgunate	148
The new Civil Code	148
Difference of age between the adopter and the adopted	148
Roman law	148
Modern European laws	149
The Taihō Code	149
The Tokugawa Shōgunate	149
The new Civil Code	150
Age of the adopted	150
Prohibition of adopting a stranger	151
The Taihō Code	151
The Tokugawa Shōgunate	151
Reason of the prohibition	151
Consequence of the prohibition	152
Increase of *rōnin*	152
Plot of Yui-no Shōsetsu	152
Reform of the law	153
Failure of male issue	154
The Taihō Code	154
The new Civil Code	154
Muko-yōshi, or "adoption of son-in-law"	154
Marriage of the adopted son with the "house-daughter"	156
Consent of the house-head and the parents	157
Effect of adoption	157

CHAPTER IX

THE DISSOLUTION OF ADOPTION

	PAGE
Two kinds of dissolution	159
Consensual dissolution	159
Judicial dissolution	159
Legal causes of dissolution	159
Disgracing the family name	159
Divorce in the case of *muko-yōshi*	160
Divorce in the case of marriage with the "house-daughter"	160

CHAPTER X

SUCCESSION

Three stages of its evolution	163
Succession to worship	163
Succession to status	163
Succession to property	163
Succession to house-worship	164
The Taihō Code	164
The Ryō-no-gigé	164
Succession to house-headship	165
Katoku as house-authority	165
Katoku as presumptive heir to house-headship	165
Katoku as house-property	167
Katoku and *familia*	167
Change in the nature of house-headship	168
Relations of the three kinds of succession	169
Succession to property	170
House-member's incapacity before the Restoration	170

Rise of the house-member's property	171
House-member's property and *peculium*	172
Growth of individual ownership	172
Two kinds of succession	174
Succession to house-headship	174
Succession to property	174
Four kinds of heirs	174
Legal heir	174
Appointed heir	174
Chosen heir	174
Ascendant heir	174
Duty of the legal heir to succeed	175
Disinheritance of an heir	176
Causes of disinheritance	176
Appointment of an heir	177
Choice of an heir	178
Ascendant's right of succession	178
Prevention of the extinction of the house	178
APPENDIX I. Prof. Westlake's letter to the author	181
APPENDIX II. A review of "Ancestor worship and Japanese Law" and "Lectures on the Japanese Civil Code"	183
EDITOR'S NOTE	187

LIST OF ILLUSTRATIONS

The author in his forty-sixth year (1900) .	*Frontispiece*
Kamidana, or the god-shelf	*To face* p. 30
Butsudan, or the Buddhist altar	,, ,, 32
The Great Shrine at Isé, dedicated to the First Imperial Ancestor	,, ,, 36
Kashihara-no Miya, dedicated to Jimmu Tennō, the First Emperor	,, ,, 40
Shrine of Kasuga, tutelary god of the Fujiwara Clan, in Nara	,, ,, 50
Shrine of Hachiman, tutelary god of the Minamoto Clan, in Kamakura	,, ,, 52
Ceremony of Shintō worship in the graveyard	,, ,, 56
Ceremony of Shintō worship in the house .	,, ,, 58
Shintō offerings before the tomb	,, ,, 66
Shintō offerings before the coffin	,, ,, 68

ANCESTOR-WORSHIP
AND
JAPANESE LAW

INTRODUCTION

In Europe and America, Ancestor-worship has long since ceased to exist, even if it was ever practised at all on those continents. In Japan—where at the present time, a constitutional government is established; where codes of laws modelled upon those of Western countries are in operation; where, in short, almost every art of civilization has taken firm root—the worshipping of deceased ancestors still obtains, and still exercises a powerful influence over the laws and customs of the people. The practice dates back to the earliest days of our history and has survived through hundreds of generations, in spite of many political and social revolutions which have taken place since the foundation of the Empire. The introduction of *Chinese civilization* into the country was favourable to the growth of this custom, by reason of the fact that the morality, laws and institutions of China are also based upon the doctrine of Ancestor-worship. *Buddhism*, which is not based upon this doctrine, but is, on the contrary, antagonistic to it, was compelled to yield to the deep-rooted belief of the people, and wisely adapted itself to the national practice; while the introduction of *Western civilization*, which has brought about so many social and political changes during the last forty years, has had no influence whatever in the direction of modifying the custom. Thus, it will be seen that the three *foreign elements*—Confucianism, Buddhism, and Western civilization—all of which have had immense influence upon our laws, manners and customs, and two of which are diametrically opposed to Ancestor-worship, could not make way against, nor put an end to, the wide-spread and persistent faith of the people.

To the Western eyes, the sight must appear strange of a Japanese family inviting their relatives, through the medium of telephone, to take part in a ceremony of this nature. Equally incongruous may seem the spectacle of members of a family, some of them attired in European and others in native costume, assembled in a room lighted by electricity, making offerings and obeisances before the memorial tablet of their ancestor. The curious blending of the Past and Present is one of the most striking phenomena of Japan. The people, whether the Shintōists or the Buddhists, are all ancestor-worshippers, and it is for that reason that I venture to approach a subject which has already been most ably dealt with by such distinguished scholars and men of letters as Fustel de Coulanges, Sir Henry Maine, Herbert Spencer, Rudolf von Ihering, Lord Avebury, Dr. Tylor, Dr. W. E. Hearn and others, whose profound investigations have thrown so much light upon the subject.

The masterly manner in which these writers have grasped the inwardness of a custom, which is totally foreign to them, is little short of marvellous, and their writings leave little room for further investigations. They have, however, observed the phenomena from *without*; and it may, perhaps, be of some interest to examine the subject from *within*, and to discuss it from the point of view of an ancestor-worshipper himself.

Before entering upon the main subject of this essay, it will be advisable to say a few words relating to Ancestor-worship in general, and to Japanese Ancestor-worship in particular.

PART I

ANCESTOR-WORSHIP IN GENERAL

ANCESTOR-WORSHIP IN GENERAL

CHAPTER I

THE ORIGIN OF ANCESTOR-WORSHIP

The origin of Ancestor-worship has been ascribed by many eminent writers to the *dread of ghosts*; and the sacrifices are said to have been offered to the souls of ancestors for the purpose of *propitiating* them.[1] Lord Avebury, for instance, says that " the worship of ancestors is a natural development of the dread of ghosts."[2] Ihering is still more explicit in his view, and denies in strong terms that Ancestor-worship is the outcome of filial devotion. His words, translated into English, run thus :—" According to the current view, the sacrifice to the dead bears testimony to the deep affection of children for

---

1. Herbert Spencer, *Principles of Sociology*, 1, §§ 146, 147, 206.
2. Lubbock, *Origin of Civilization*, 5th ed., p. 322.

their parents. This might be conceded, did we not know how the son treated his parents during their lifetime. But what is the sacrifice to the dead—the mean gift of food and drink which from time to time is placed upon the grave —when compared with the fate to which the son submits his parents during their lifetime, and to which he is legally entitled to submit them? A strange love, indeed, which needed to be kindled by death, and which offered to the parents on the other side of the grave the bread which was either denied or given grudgingly to them on this side! It is not *love*, indeed, but *fear*, which prompted the sacrifice to the dead. * * * * * It is the duty of the descendants to bring food and drink to the grave of their departed; should this be neglected, the dead will avenge themselves, and appear as threatening spectres to inflict all kinds of trouble and evil upon those who neglect them.

"This is, I believe, the original motive of the sacrifice to the dead; it is not the outcome of

THE ORIGIN OF ANCESTOR-WORSHIP 9

filial devotion and love, but of *egoism*, i. e., *fear* and *dread*."[1]

With the greatest deference due to these writers, I cannot persuade myself to accept their view. It appears to me more correct to attribute the origin of Ancestor-worship to a contrary cause. It was the *love* of ancestors, not the *dread* of them, which gave rise to the custom of worshipping and making offerings of food and drink to their spirits. I cannot understand why a primitive people, who must have loved their parents in their lifetime, should have experienced fear of them after their death. I cannot understand why a primitive people should have been so near-sighted and thoughtless as to ill-treat their parents without scruple during their lifetime, and suddenly begin to fear their spirits after their death. Why did they not entertain any apprehension that they would

---

[1] Ihering, *Vorgeschichte der Indoeuropäer*, S. 59. (translated into English by Drucker under the title of *The Evolution of the Aryan*, § 13.)

be avenged by their parents' ghosts for their unkindness towards them? Ghosts are usually conceived as being endowed with memory and as requiting good or evil done to them during their lifetime. Why do they, then, avenge themselves only for the neglect of giving them food and drink after their death, when, perhaps, they are less needed, and not for the denial of them during life, when, surely, they were most needed? " A strange *fear*, indeed,"—I am tempted to say, substituting only one word for that of Ihering—" which needed to be kindled by death, and which offered to the parents on the other side of the grave the bread which was either denied or given grudgingly to them on this side ! "

It is true that the treatment of the aged is, in one sense, an index to the grade of civilization to which any people has attained, and respect for age is the result of a very slow growth. It is also well known that among peoples of lower grade, the practice of exposing to death

THE ORIGIN OF ANCESTOR-WORSHIP

or otherwise disposing of the aged or infirm was very common[1]; but it is a mistake to conclude from it, as the great jurist seems to do, that they did not love and honour their parents. The prevalence, among primitive peoples, of the practice of exposing or putting the aged or infirm to death does not show that they were destitute of filial devotion, any more than the existence of the custom of abortion shows the want of parental love among the people. They were forced to it by the dire necessity of hunger in time of famine, or compelled to it by the stern necessities of war, as the aged or infirm were felt to be not only a drain upon the scanty food supplies, but an embarrassment in time of war.[2] They would have certainly honoured their old parents as they do now, did not the cruel necessity of the primitive struggle for existence force them to quench the natural

---

1. See Hartwell Jones, *The Dawn of European Civilization*, ch. xiv; also the present author's work 隱居論 (*On the Abdication of the House-headship*).
2. Hartwell Jones, *loc. cit.*, ch. xiv.

instinct of pity, and very often invent superstitious reasons for these barbarous practices in order to console their guilty conscience. If there were any tribe or race more destitute of filial devotion or parental love than others, that tribe or race would surely first die out in the struggle for existence.[1] If mankind in their primitive stage had been entirely destitute of filial devotion or parental love, if their life had been the life of egoism and not of love and sympathy, the human race would have been extinct long ago, and this world would have become the world of wolves and tigers.

Respect for their parents may, indeed, in some cases have become akin to *awe*; yet it was *love, not dread*, which caused this feeling of awe. A Chinese philosopher Chu-hsi (朱熹) accurately summarizes the origin of Ancestor-worship when he says in his " Book of House-Ceremonies " (家禮) that " the object of worship

---

[1]. E. T. Seton, *The Natural History of the Ten Commandments*, pp. 7-11.

is nothing else than performing all that is dictated by a *feeling of true love and respect*" (凡祭主於盡愛敬之誠而已), while the late Professor Kurita (栗田寬) begins his book on "The Rituals of Worship" (祭典私攷) with these words:—"Who, endowed with life in this world, has not a mind to honour his parents? Who, honouring his parents, does not reverence his ancestors? Who, honouring parents and reverencing ancestors, is not prompted to follow the dictates of affectionate sentiment by offering sacrifices to their spirits? This is the outcome of the faculty of intelligence that is implanted in human nature, and through it arose the ceremonies of offering sacrifices to spirits from the Age of the Gods." He continues:—"Those who are left behind in this world by their parents feel pangs of grief in their hearts as months and years pass away. When the flowers begin to blossom in the spring, when trees and grasses put forth their luxuriance in the summer, when insects sing in the autumn evenings, and when the winter brings its dews and frosts, everything they see and hear, stirs up a feeling of sorrow, and reminds them of bygone days when their parents walked the earth; and to their inability to forget their parents is due the practice of offering them food and drink. Thus, the custom of making sacrifices to spirits finds its origin in human nature." In like manner, Baron Junjirō Hosokawa (細川潤次郎) in his "Lectures on National Festival Days," (祝祭日講話) explains the source of the festivals set apart for sacrifice to the Imperial Ancestors.

The writers who attribute the origin of Ancestor-worship to "*the dread of ghosts*" and to "*ghost-propitiation*" fail to discriminate between ghosts which are to be *dreaded* and those which are to be *respected*. Ghosts can be divided into *two* separate classes, those that compel *fear* and those that inspire *love* and *respect*. The Romans seem to have made a similar distinction, for they had different names for the two kinds of spirits; the *Manes* being called *Larvae* when they were malignant, and *Lares* when they were benevolent and propitious[1]. The ghosts of enemies or of those that have met with an unnatural death belong to the former; and sacrifices are sometimes offered to their spirits for the purpose of propitiating them. But the ghosts of ancestors belong to the latter class; and sacrifices are offered to them, and their spirits are worshipped, as a result of love and respect which their descendants feel towards them. This practice arises out of the natural impulse of kinsmen to provide their dead relatives with food, drink and clothing, as in the days of their life. Confucius (孔子) is represented by his disciples as having made offerings to the souls of his ancestors just as if they were living. (祭如在)[2] That great Oriental sage says:—"It is the highest filial piety for offspring to serve the dead as they would serve the living, and to serve the departed as they would serve the present." (事死如事生事亡如事存, 孝之至也)[3]

---

1. Fustel de Coulanges, *La Cité Antique*, liv. 1, ch. ii.
2. 論語 (*The Analects of Confucius.*)
3. 中庸 (*The Doctrine of the Mean.*)

We celebrate the anniversary of our ancestors, pay visits to their graves, offer flowers, food and drink, burn incense, and bow before their tombs entirely from a feeling of love and respect for their memory, and no idea of " dread " enters our minds in doing so. Moreover, in the records and traditions of our country, there is nothing which suggests that ancestors were worshipped with a view to propitiating their souls.

I do not wonder at all that Westerners should entertain different notions about ghosts from what other less civilized peoples have of them, for they have been so long free from the superstitions of this kind, and so far away from the time when they had the practice of Ancestor-worship,[1] that they are less familiar, so to speak, with ghosts and should therefore naturally regard them as objects of horror and dread. When I was a student in London, I once went to the Lyceum Theatre to see Henry Irving play

---

[1]. W. E. Hearn, *Aryan Household*, ch. ii, §2 ; Tylor, *Primitive Culture*, II, ch. xiv ; Spencer, *Principles of Sociology*, I, §152.

Hamlet. I admired indeed the performance of that famous actor; but when it came to the ghost scene, I was struck with an impression that our actors would perform it in a different way. Hamlet, as represented by Irving, appeared to me as constantly showing signs of fear and dread, not only on account of the horrible story told by his father's ghost—which is but natural—but for the ghost itself. A Japanese actor, if he were to act the part of Hamlet, would certainly show strong marks of love and respect towards the father's spirit, mingled with the feeling of sorrow and sympathy for his father's fate, and of horror and anger at the "foul and most unnatural murder." He would perhaps try to embrace the phantom instead of parrying, as the great English actor did. Of course, I by no means say that this is the proper way of representing Shakespeare's famous play; nor do I presume to think that I understood Irving's acting well. I only state my impression. Ghost scenes are not uncommon in Japanese theatres;

and when the ghost appears to the parent, sons, daughters, friends or lovers, those who meet it never show signs of dread, but those of joy for the meeting, mingled perhaps with sorrow and sympathy.

I am glad to have found, after I had brought out the first edition of this book, that one of the greatest authorities on anthropology holds a similar view on the subject. Dr. Tylor says :—" Happily for man's anticipation of death, and for the treatment of the sick and aged, thoughts of horror and hatred do not preponderate in ideas of deified ancestors, who are regarded on the whole as kindly patron spirits, at least to their own kinsfolk and worshippers."[1]

The theory of the "dread of ghosts" and "ghost-propitiation" seems absolutely unnatural so far as the worship of ancestors is concerned; and, however strange the expression may sound

---

1. Tylor, *Primitive Culture*, II, ch. xiv. Also cf. the following passage from the same author :—"... respect to the living ancestor passes into his worship as an ancestral spirit." (Tylor, *Anthropology*, p. 410.)

to the Western ears, I deem it nearer the truth to say that it was the "*Love of Ghosts*" which gave rise to the custom of Ancestor-worship.

CHAPTER II

Ancestor-Worship as the Origin of Social Life

What was the bond which originally united men into a homogeneous social life? At the present time, there is a decided tendency on the part of men to form themselves into communities with the object of attaining collectively some *common end*. Some establish religious congregations in support of a common creed; some found scientific associations for the acquirement of common knowledge; others found commercial corporations for their mutual benefit; while others again group themselves into political parties with the object of winning recognition for their particular political convictions. The number of social communities is steadily increasing and their influence becomes more and more wide-spread with the progress of civilization. Every day, men are becoming more alive to the advantages of co-operation and the benefits arising from union in every branch of life. The sphere of these social groups even shows signs of overstepping the boundaries of States and the limits of races, and in these brotherhoods of men occupying a position in the higher stages of civilization, there is always to be found certain *conscious aims* which form the bond of their union.

But primitive men were ignorant of the advantages resulting from combination, and moreover, those virtues which are essential to the maintenance of society were not yet developed among them. The initial bond of union among primitive men must, then, be sought for in some *unconscious force*, and there can be little doubt that it had its origin in the ties of *consanguinity*. It is most natural that children born of and reared by, the same mother should live together. They would, when they grow up, hunt together in the wood for their game, fight abreast in the field with their common enemies, avenge the death of their kinsmen, and help one another in getting their food, clothing and habitation. The children of these brothers and sisters would usually do the same, and the next generation would most probably follow the examples of their predecessors. Thus, the most natural basis for the beginning of man's social group is the *unity of blood*. But the sphere of love amongst kinsmen is *limited in extent*. The social group in the first generation, consisting of brothers and sisters, including their parents if living, would be a very compact body, closely held together by a strong tie of fraternal and sisterly affection. But the next group consisting of cousins, would be a looser body compared with the first, as the tie of love and sympathy among them is not so strong as among brothers and sisters. The third generation would be a still looser body. The feeling of kinship obligation becomes continually weaker, as the degree of consanguinity becomes more remote and the number of kinsmen more numerous.

There must have been, therefore, some other factor that acted as the centripetal force which drew distant relatives together and bound them into a community. *That factor was Ancestor-worship.* The worship of common ancestors, and the ceremonies connected therewith, kept alive the memory of a common descent amongst a large number of widely scattered kinsmen, who were so far removed from one another that they would, without this link, have fallen away from family intercourse. As the sentiment of consanguinity, which has been shown to have been the only bond of union amongst primitive men, grew looser by the wider dispersal of the ever-increasing members of a family, the necessity became greater to weld together the various units of kindred lineage by means of the worship of a common progenitor, in order that the primitive group might grow up into a homogeneous community. Now, if the primary bond of union was the tie of blood, and if the tie of blood means the *extension of sympathy and love* to distant kinsmen, the explanation which has been given of the origin of Ancestor-worship seems to accord better with the effect of this practice, than does the theory of the "dread of ghosts" or "ghost-propitiation."

The question whether Ancestor-worship is *a universal institution*, that is to say, whether all races of mankind have, at some time or other, passed, or must pass, through the stage of this worship is one, the solution of which cannot be lightly attempted. Personally, I can not conceive how the human race could have arrived at its present state of social and political life without at first experiencing the influence of Ancestor-worship. Dr. Tylor says:—"Manes-worship is one of the great branches of the religion of mankind. Its principles are not difficult to understand, for they plainly keep up the social relation of the living world."[1] Sir Henry Maine also asserts that Ancestor-worship is still the practical religion of much

---

1. Tylor, *Primitive Culture*, II, ch. xiv.

THE ORIGIN OF SOCIAL LIFE

the largest part of the human race.[1] According to Coulanges, the custom existed both in Greece and in Rome[2]; and Dr. Hearn shows that Aryans were an ancestor-worshipping race[3]; while most of the recent investigations of historians and sociologists[4], as well as travellers' accounts of the manners and customs of primitive peoples prove that the worship of deceased ancestors is practised by a very large proportion of mankind. This seems to point to the conclusion that all races practise it in the infancy of their development, and that it was the first step towards the inauguration of social life on a wide basis.

---

1. Maine, *Early Law and Custom*, ch. iii.
2. F. de Coulanges, *La Cité Antique*.
3. Hearn, *Aryan Household*.
4. See particularly Dr. Steinmetz's *Ethnologische Studien zur Ersten Entwickelung der Strafe*.

PART II

ANCESTOR-WORSHIP IN JAPAN

ANCESTOR-WORSHIP IN JAPAN

I now proceed to describe the present condition of Ancestor-worship in Japan. It was the primeval religion of the country from the earliest times of our history and is universally practised by the people at the present moment. As has already been pointed out at the commencement of this book, neither the introduction of Chinese civilization, the spread of Buddhism nor the influence of European civilization has done anything to shake the firm-rooted custom of the people.

CHAPTER I

THREE KINDS OF ANCESTOR-WORSHIP

There are two sacred places in every Japanese house: the *Kamidana* (神棚), or "god-shelf"; and the *Butsudan* (佛壇), or "Buddhist altar." The first-named is the Shintō altar which is a plain wooden shelf. In the centre of this sacred shelf is placed a *Taima* or *Ō-nusa* "great offering" (大麻) which is part of the offerings made to the Daijingū of Isé (伊勢大神宮), or temple dedicated to Amaterasu Ō-Mikami (天照皇大神), the *First Imperial Ancestor*. The *Taima* is distributed from the Temple of Isé to every house in the Empire at the end of each year and is worshipped by every loyal Japanese as the representation of the First Imperial Ancestor. On this altar, the offerings of rice, saké (liquor brewed from rice), and branches of *sakaki*-tree (*Cleyera japonica*) are usually placed, and every morning the members of the household make reverential obeisance

KAMIDANA, OR THE GOD-SHELF

before it by clapping hands and bowing, while in the evening lights are also placed on the shelf. On this shelf is placed, in addition, the charm of *ujigami* (氏神), or the *local tutelary god* of the family, and, in many houses, the charms of the other Shintō deities also.

In the Shintō household there is a second " god-shelf," or *Kamidana*, which is dedicated exclusively to the worship of *the ancestors of the house*. On this second shelf are placed cenotaphs, bearing the names of the ancestors, their ages, and the dates of their deaths. These memorial tablets are called *Mitamashiro* which means " representatives of souls," and they are usually placed in small boxes shaped like Shintō shrines. Offerings of rice, saké, fish, *sakaki*-tree and lamps are made on this second shelf as on the first.

In the Buddhist household there is, in addition to the *Kamidana*, a *Butsudan*, on which are placed cenotaphs, bearing on the front posthumous Buddhist names, and on the back the names borne by the ancestors during their lifetime. The cenotaph is usually lacquered and gilded, having a lotus flower as pedestal, and is sometimes placed in a box called *Zushi*, while family crests are very often painted both on the tablet and on the box. Offerings of flowers, branches of *shikimi*-tree (*Illicium religiosum*), tea, cakes, rice and other vegetable foods, are usually placed before the cenotaphs, while incense is continually burnt; and in the evening, small lamps are lighted. The *Butsudan* takes the place of the second- "god-shelf" of the Shintō household, both being dedicated to the worship of family ancestors.

From the foregoing brief description of the sacred altars of a Japanese household, it will be seen that there are *three kinds of Ancestor-worship* in vogue: namely, the worship of the First Imperial Ancestor by the people; the worship of the patron god of the locality, which, as I shall show later on, is a relic of the worship of clan-ancestors by clansmen; and the worship of the family ancestors by members of the household.

BUTSUDAN, OR THE BUDDHIST ALTAR

CHAPTER II

THE WORSHIP OF THE IMPERIAL ANCESTORS

The first of the three kinds of Ancestor-worship, namely, homage to the Imperial Ancestors, and especially to the First Imperial Ancestor, Amaterasu Ō-Mikami, or " The Great Goddess of the Celestial Light," may be styled the national worship. The places set apart for religious exercises in honour of the First Imperial Ancestor are three in number: the Temple of Daijingū at Isé, the Kashiko-Dokoro (賢所) in the Sanctuary of the Imperial Palace, and *Kamidana*, which is to be found in every house. In the two first-named, the Divine Mirror, the original and its duplicate respectively, represents the Imperial Ancestor. This is the mirror which, according to old histories, Amaterasu Ō-Mikami gave to her grandson Ninigi-no Mikoto (瓊瓊杵尊), accompanied by the injunction that her descendants should look upon that mirror as representing her soul, and should worship it as herself. The Divine Mirror, called "Yata-no-Kagami" (八咫鏡), was kept and worshipped in the Imperial Palace down to the sixth year of the reign of Sujin (崇神) (92 B. C.), when the Emperor, fearing lest familiarity with it might engender disrespect, ordered Princess Toyo-sukiirihime-no-Mikoto (豐鍬入姫命) to set up a temple in the village of Kasanui in the province of Yamato and decreed that the mirror should be housed and worshipped there. This temple was afterward removed to various localities, until Isé was finally chosen as its permanent site. The Emperor further caused a duplicate of the mirror to be made and placed in the Sanctuary of the Palace in order that he and his descendants might worship as heretofore. Thus, the original mirror is now in the Daijingū or the Great Shrine at Isé, and the duplicate in the Temple of the Kashiko-Dokoro in the Imperial Sanctuary. The Great Shrine at Isé is held in special reverence. A new shrine is built, and the old one taken down, every twenty years, in accordance with an immemorial usage. Anciently, on the accession of each Emperor, a virgin Imperial Princess was appointed Lady Guardian (齋王) of the Shrine; but now a Prince of the Blood is appointed to the sacred post of Lord Guardian of the Great Shrine at Isé.

At the present time, not only does every loyal Japanese worship Daijingū in his own house, but many look upon it as a duty to make a pilgrimage to Isé, or "Isé-Mairi" (伊勢參宮), at least once during his lifetime. Thousands of people, high and low, rich and poor, yearly throng the temple of Daijingū from all parts of the country, and offer the holy music and dance called "Dai-dai-Kagura" in honour of the First Imperial Ancestor. It is said that in recent years more than ten thousand people visit Isé every New Year's Day to pay their respect to the Great Shrine. There is a curious custom, which, however, has greatly declined of late, known as "nukémairi," or "truant pilgrimage," in accordance with which shop-boys and village youths set out on a secret pilgrimage to Isé without obtaining the permission of their masters or parents. It may be mentioned, in passing, that these disciplinary lapses are not usually punished as such acts would be under ordinary circumstances. These pilgrimages are frequently undertaken without any provision whatever for the journey, but as the youthful pilgrims are easily distinguishable from ordinary beggars, there are plenty of kind-hearted persons ready and willing to offer them food, money and, sometimes, even shelter.

In the Sanctuary of the Imperial Palace there are three temples—Kashiko-Dokoro (賢所), Kwōrei-Den (皇靈殿) and Shin-Den (神殿). The Kashiko-Dokoro where the Divine Mirror is placed occupies the central position and is dedicated to the worship of the First Imperial Ancestor. The Kwōrei-Den stands to the west of the Kashiko-Dokoro, and is dedicated to the worship of all the Imperial Ancestors since Jimmu Ten-

The Great Shrine at Isé, dedicated to the First Imperial Ancestor

nō (神武天皇), the first Emperor and the founder of the Empire. The third temple, Shin-Den, stands to the east of the Kashiko-Dokoro, and serves to honour all the other deities. It is in this Sanctuary of the Imperial Palace that the ceremonies of the Festivals below mentioned are held.

The Imperial House Ordinance relating to Festivals (皇室祭祀令), which was promulgated in 1902, contains minute regulations as to the ceremony of worship in the Imperial House. The Festivals are divided into the Great Festivals and the Small Festivals. The distinction between these two classes of Festivals consists in this, that in the former, the ceremonies are conducted by the Emperor in person, while in the latter, the Emperor only worships, the rest of the ceremony being performed by the Master of the Rituals.

According to this Ordinance, there are thirteen Great Festivals and eight Small Festivals. I will briefly explain each of them.

The first Great Festival takes place on the 3rd of January, and is called Genshi Sai (元始祭), or the "Festival of the Sacrifice to the Origin." The Emperor, attended by the Princes of the Blood and all the high officials of the *Shin-nin* and *Choku-nin* ranks, makes offerings in person and reads prayers in the Three Temples of the Sanctuary at ten o'clock in the morning; and after the Emperor retires, the Princes of the Blood and the high officials worship the Three Temples in the order of their rank and precedence. The ceremony of worship is held by the Empress and the Crown Prince at eleven o'clock, and by all the Peers and officials of the *Sō-nin* rank from noon till two o'clock in the afternoon. The meaning of this festival is said to be that the Three Temples represent directly or indirectly the *origin of the Imperial Throne*, and that the Festival is held in the beginning of the year in order to remember and show gratitude towards the "Origin," or the First and other Imperial Ancestors and other deities, before all other affairs of the State are transacted.[1]

The second Great Festival takes place on the 11th of February, and is called Kigensetsu (紀元節), or the anniversary of the accession of the first Emperor and the foundation of the Empire. This is considered to be the greatest Festival of the year; and many important events of the State, such as the promulgation of the Constitution and the Imperial House Law took place on that day. After the ceremonies are performed at the Kwōrei-Den, a grand banquet is given in the Palace to the Princes of the Blood, foreign ministers, high officials and nobles.

The third Great Festival is Shunki Kwōrei Sai (春季皇靈祭), or "the Spring Sacrifice to the Spirits of the Imperial Ancestors," and takes place on the day of the vernal equinox. The ceremony of worship is performed in the Kwōrei-Den by the Emperor in person and is nearly

---

[1] 細川潤次郎著　祝祭日講話 (Baron J. Hosokawa, *Lectures on the Festival Days.*)

similar to that of other Great Festivals.

On the same day, the fourth Great Festival takes place, which is called Shunki Shin-Den Sai (春季神殿祭), or the "Spring Sacrifice to the Shrines of Gods." The ceremonies of this Festival are performed in the Shin-Den.

The fifth Great Festival is Jimmu Tennō Sai (神武天皇祭). This takes place on the 3rd of April, for this day is the anniversary of the death of the First Emperor.

The sixth and seventh Great Festivals are held on the same day, that is, the day of the autumnal equinox. The former is Shūki Kwōrei Sai (秋季皇靈祭), or the "Autumnal Sacrifice to the Spirits of the Imperial Ancestors," and the latter Shūki Shin-Den Sai (秋季神殿祭), or the "Autumnal Sacrifice to the Shrines of Gods." They correspond in every respect to those which take place on the vernal equinox.

The 17th of October is the date of the eighth Great Festival, which is called Shinshō Sai, or Kannamé Matsuri (神嘗祭). The principal cere-

KASHIHARA-NO MIYA, dedicated to Jimmu Tennō, the First Emperor

mony of this Festival consists in offering the first-fruits of the year to the First Imperial Ancestor. The ceremonies are performed both at the Great Shrine at Isé and at the Kashiko-Dokoro. On this occasion, the Emperor also performs the ceremony called *Yō-hai*, or the "Distant worship," of the First Imperial Ancestor, and sends an Imperial messenger for offering sacrifices to the Great Shrine at Isé. With the new crops, *Nozaki-no-nusa*, or the "Sacrifice of the First Tribute," an offering of silk, is made. This is said to be a relic of the ancient practice of selecting the best portion of the "first instalment" of the taxes in kind, and making an offering of it on the graves of the Imperial Ancestors.

Next comes the ninth Great Festival, Shinshō Sai or Nii-namé Matsuri (新嘗祭), which is the festival of the feast of the new crop of rice. The offering of the new rice is made to the First and other Imperial Ancestors and other deities at the Sanctuary of the Imperial Palace. The

Emperor partakes of the new rice and feasts are given to the Princes of the Blood, high officials and nobles. The feast commences on the night of the 23rd of November and ends on the morning of the 24th.

The tenth Great Festival is Sen-Tei-Sai (先帝祭), or the anniversary of the death of the late Emperor.

The eleventh Great Festival is the Shiki-nen Sai (式年祭), or the "Celebration Year's Festival" of the Emperors within three generations previous to the last Emperor.

The twelfth Great Festival is the Shiki-nen Sai, or the "Celebration Year's Festival" of the late Empress, who was the consort of the late Emperor.

The thirteenth Great Festival is the Shiki-nen Sai, or the "Celebration Year's Festival" of the late Empress, who was the Mother of the reigning Emperor.

The "Celebration Years" above mentioned, are the third, fifth, tenth, twentieth, thirtieth, fortieth, and fiftieth years from the date of a death, and every hundredth year afterward.

The Small Festivals are eight in number:—

1. Sai-tan Sai (歳旦祭), or the "New Year's Festival," which takes place at the Three Temples in the Sanctuary of the Imperial Palace. Before the ceremony of Sai-tan Sai is commenced, the Emperor performs the ceremony of *Shihō-hai* (四方拜), or the "Worshipping in Four Directions." This takes place in the Imperial Palace at four o'clock on the morning of the first day of the year. The Emperor begins by worshipping the First Imperial Ancestor in the direction of the west, and then in the directions of the respective graves of the First Emperor Jimmu Tennō and the Imperial Father, and of the shrines of other deities. The Emperor then performs the ceremony of worship at the Three Temples. After the above ceremonies are over, the New Year's Audience is held in the Imperial Palace, in which the Emperor and the Empress receive New Year's congratulations from mem-

bers of the Imperial Family, foreign ministers, officials, nobles and other dignitaries; so that the first ceremony of Court may be said to begin with the worship of the Imperial Ancestors.

2. Kinen Sai (祈年祭), or the "Festival of the Prayer for the Year's Crop." This takes place on the 17th of February in the Three Temples of the Imperial Sanctuary, and sacrifices are offered to the Great Shrine at Isé and other shrines.

3. The Kashiko-Dokoro O-Kagura (賢所御神樂), which takes place in the middle of December, when the Sacred Music is played before the Temple of the First Imperial Ancestor.

4. Tenchō-Setsu Sai (天長節祭), or the "Festival of the Emperor's Birthday."

5. The Rei Sai (例祭), or the "Annual Festival" for the worship of the Emperors within three generations previous to the last Emperor.

6. The Rei Sai, or the "Annual Festival" for the worship of the late Empress, who was the consort of the late Emperor.

THE WORSHIP OF IMPERIAL ANCESTORS 45

7. The Rei Sai, or the "Annual Festival" for the worship of the late Empress, who was the Mother of the reigning Emperor.

The Rei Sai above mentioned takes place every year on the day of the month corresponding to the date of the death of the Emperor or Empress respectively.

8. The Shiki-nen Sai, or the "Celebration Year's Festival" of all the Emperors excluding the First Emperor Jimmu Tennō and the Emperors within three generations from the last Emperor, for the anniversary of the death of the Emperors last mentioned are celebrated as Great Festivals.

It will be observed that all of the Festivals above mentioned relate to the worship of the Imperial Ancestors. They are, therefore, religious observances belonging to the Imperial House. But at the same time, all of the Great Festival Days and two of the Small Festival Days, that is, New Year's Day and the Emperor's Birthday, are observed as national holidays. National flags representing the Rising Sun are hung out at every house; women don their best attire, and the streets are thronged with holiday-makers; while children go to their schools and assemble before the portraits of the Emperor and the Empress, and Meiji Tennō's famous Rescript on Education is read and explained to them by the schoolmasters.

From the foregoing, it will be readily seen that the *worship of the Imperial Ancestors is the national worship*.

CHAPTER III

THE WORSHIP OF CLAN-ANCESTORS

The population of Japan is considered originally to have been divided into *three classes*: *Shin-betsu* (神別), or the "Divine branch," which consisted of the descendants of gods; *Kwō-betsu* (皇別), or the "Imperial branch," which included the descendants of the Imperial families; and *Ban-betsu* (番別), or the "foreign branch," comprising the descendants of naturalized foreigners. Each of these three branches was divided again into many clans, each having a distinctive clan-name *uji* (氏) or *kabane* (姓). With regard to the original signification of the words *uji* and *kabane*, there is considerable divergence of opinion among Japanese scholars. Some maintain that the word came from *umi-chi* (生血), or "blood of birth"; others derive it from *izu* (出), or "origin"; while the claims of *uchi* (內) "house" also receive support in certain quarters (拾芥抄).

As to the derivation of the word *kabane*, which was sometimes used to denote clan-names, almost equally divergent views exist. Some suggest *agamayena* (あがまへな), or "reverential name" in view of the fact that the word was more usually employed to convey the meaning of a title of honour; others derive it from *kami hone* (神骨), or "god's bone," the word signifying that a clan-name is like the bone of the ancestor which remains after his death; while not a few are in favour of applying its ordinary meaning, namely "corpse," because it is a corpse that descendants succeed. The late Professor Kurita, in his learned dissertation on the subject of clans (氏族考), derived it from *kabuné* (頭根), "root" or "stock," the word being employed to designate the root or stock from which descendants sprang. I have no desire, however, to involve myself in an etymological discussion as to the original signification of these words; nor is it within the scope of this book to do so. No matter which of these disputed derivations

THE WORSHIP OF CLAN-ANCESTORS 49

be the correct one, they one and all convey the idea of a certain *common ancestor*, and consequently of the *community of blood*.

The word *uji* denoted the clan-name, or the common appellation of the descendants of the same ancestor, and sometimes the clan itself. The word *kabane* was more usually employed to designate titles of honour, but was also sometimes employed in the sense of a clan-name. In course of time, each *uji*, or clan, was subdivided into smaller clans, and hence arose the division of *uji* into *ō-uji* (大氏), the " great clan " and *ko-uji* (小氏), the " small clan." Each *ō-uji* consisted of a number of subordinate bodies, and usually certain words were added to great-clan names, in order to distinguish the sub-clans from the parent community; for example, Nakatomi (中臣) was a great-clan name, borne by the descendants of Ama-no-Koyane-no Mikoto (天兒屋根命), from which sprang the subdivisions Nakatomi-no-Sakahito (中臣酒人), Nakatomi-no-Miyatoko (中臣宮處), Nakatomi-no-Ōya (中臣大家), etc.

Each clan has a clan-god or *uji-gami* (氏神), who is the eponym of that particular community; thus, Kasuga is the famous *uji-gami* of the Fujiwara Clan which was one of the largest and most influential clans in Japan. In early times, it seems to have been customary to render homage to the clan-god every month at the house of each individual clansman (宅神祭); but afterwards this practice declined, and festivals in honour of the clan-ancestor were substituted, and these were held three times a year in the temple. All clansmen took part in the ceremony, and records still exist which show that court-officials were permitted to set out on a journey to attend the festival of the clan-god or ancestor, without first obtaining leave of absence, when the ceremony was performed in a place far away from the capital. Sometimes lands were presented by the Emperors to the temples of clan-gods of high officials, in order to mitigate the heavy expenses of festivals. The offerings made on the occasion of festivals usual-

Shrine of Kasuga, Tutelary God of the Fujiwara Clan, in Nara

ly consisted of food, drink and clothing. In order to give an idea of the nature of the oblations on these occasions, I will translate literally a portion of the prayers recited during the festival of the Fujiwara clan-god:—" and the offerings hereby most respectfully presented are divine treasures in the form of a mirror, a sword, a bow, a spear and a horse; as vestments, light cloth, shining cloth, soft cloth (silk), coarse cloth (hemp); the first-fruits from the tributes of different provinces; from among the things of the blue sea, the broad-fin (large fish), narrow-fin (small fish), weeds of the deep and weeds of the shore; from among things of mountain and field, sweet herbs and pungent herbs; and tall jars filled with saké and other things all piled up like a range of mountains. These things are proffered by A, the master of the sacra, as the grand offering, the peaceful offering and the full offering, and he reverently prays that the Divine Spirits may accept them peacefully." Sometimes sacred music and dances were also offered in addition to the various articles enumerated above.

The word *uji-gami* or clan-god is now used in the same sense as *ubusuna-no-kami*, or the *local tutelary god*, or the patron-god of a man's birth-place or domicile. This change in the use of the word *uji-gami* from *clan-god* to *local tutelary god* possibly arose from the fact that in early days clansmen usually lived together in the same locality, and erected a temple for the worship of their ancestral eponyms, with the result that the clan-god and the local patron-god meant one and the same deity. But subsequently, the means of communication gradually developed and the members of the various clans began to disperse and to live in different parts of the country. Even now, it is no uncommon thing to find, in the country villages, the greater part of the inhabitants bearing the same family name. Moreover, it will be shown presently that the administrative departments of the Empire, from being *tribal*, gradually became local and *territorial*.

Shrine of Hachiman, Tutelary God of the Minamoto Clan, in Kamakura

In all parts of the Empire, persons living within certain localities are designated *uji-ko* (氏子), or the "children of the clan." They carry their children, soon after they are born, to the temple of the local patron-god for the first worship, which is called *miya-mairi*, and each *uji-ko* contributes towards the maintenance of the temples and the expenses of the festivals, which are held in honour of *uji-gami* at least twice every year.

All these facts combine to show that the worship of *uji-gami*, or local patron-gods, is a relic of the worship of clan-ancestors.

CHAPTER IV

The Worship of Family-Ancestors

The next point to be discussed is the worship of the Ancestors of a House. The occasions for the celebration of house-worship may be classed under *three categories*: the *Sacrifice-days*, the *Sacrifice-months*, and the *Sacrifice-years*. The Sacrifice-day, or *kinichi*, is the day in each month corresponding to the day of an ancestor's death. For instance, if the death occurred on the fifth day of a month, the *kinichi* would be celebrated on the fifth of every month. The Sacrifice-month, or *shō-tsuki*, is the day of the month corresponding to the day and month of an ancestor's death. Thus, if the death occurred on the fifth of September, the *shō-tsuki* would be observed on the fifth of every September. The Sacrifice-year, or *nen-ki*, is the day of the month in certain years, corresponding to the day of the month of the death of an ancestor, the ceremony of worship in connection with it usually taking place among the Shintōists on the first, fifth, tenth, twentieth, thirtieth, fortieth, fiftieth and hundredth year. After the hundredth year, the anniversary is usually celebrated every fiftieth year. Among the Buddhists, these anniversary ceremonies are usually observed on the first, third, seventh, thirteenth, seventeenth, twenty-third, twenty-seventh, thirty-third, thirty-seventh, forty-third, forty-seventh, fiftieth, and hundredth years, after which period they are held every fiftieth year as in the case of the Shintōists.

In accordance with an ancient custom, sacrifices are offered and ceremonies of worship are performed by the Buddhists, after a man's death, every seventh day until the seventh seventh day—that is the forty-ninth day from the date of death—these sacrifice-days being respectively designated the "first seventh-day," "second seventh-day" and so on. Amongst the Shintōists these Sacrifice-days are usually commemorated every tenth day after death, and end with the fiftieth or hundredth.

As a rule, on the Sacrifice-days or *kinichi* of each month, after the " seventh seventh-day " among the Buddhists, and after the fiftieth, or the one hundredth day among the Shintōists, only members of the family and near relatives take part in the proceedings ; but on the occasion of *shō-tsuki* and *nenki*, feasts are provided, and relatives and descendants of ancestors are invited to participate in the worship. In both the Shintō and Buddhist religions, priests officiate at the ceremonies, but among the Shintōists, the religious services are held in their own houses, while among the Buddhists, they sometimes take place in temples as well as in their own homes.

The Shintō rituals of worship differ somewhat from those of the Buddhist religion and there are also some variations observable in the rites of different Buddhist sects. Shintō offerings consist of saké, rice, fish, game, vegetables and fruits for food and drink, and pieces of silk

Ceremony of Shintō Worship in the Graveyard

and hemp for clothing, while branches of *sakaki*-tree and flowers are also frequently offered. The priests who perform the ceremony clap their hands before the altar, and the chief priest pronounces the prayer, or *norito* (祝詞), the words of which vary on different occasions, although, at the commencement of the recital, the spirits of the ancestors are almost invariably informed that the head of the family, with other members and connections, are assembled for the purpose of celebrating the particular anniversary, reverently offering to the sacred soul " lucks of sea and mountain " (*umi-no-sachi* 海之幸, *yama-no-sachi* 山之幸, meaning thereby fish, game, etc.), that the house is in a peaceful condition, and that the descendants are prosperous. The prayer usually concludes with the supplication that the spirit may protect and watch over the family, and accept the offerings dutifully made. After this, each of the assembled party, commencing with the head of the house, takes a *tamagushi* (玉串), or small branch of *sakaki*-tree, to which is attached a piece of paper representing *nigotayé* (和多閇), or fine cloth, places it on the altar, and then claps hands and makes obeisances. With regard to the significance of the hand-clapping, three explanations have been given. Some consider it as a sign of *joy*, others as an *invocation*, and others again, as a sign of *admiration*. The last interpretation is the opinion of the late Professor Konakamura (小中村清矩) and is most widely accepted. At the termination of this ceremony, all the relatives are invited to a banquet, concerning which the late Professor Kurita, in his " Studies in the Rituals of Worship " (祭典私改), writes ;—" The relatives assembled partake of the sacred saké, which has been offered to the ancestor, and talk about his meritorious deeds, while each person present gives voice to a resolve not to degrade in any way the good name of the ancestor."

Here I may mention the custom of " declaring name " (名乗を揚げる), in order to show in what high esteem the ancestral name was held

CEREMONY OF SHINTŌ WORSHIP IN THE HOUSE
(Chief priest reading the prayer)

THE WORSHIP OF FAMILY-ANCESTORS 59

in feudal days. The etiquette of war required that the warrior should declare his name on the battlefield and challenge the enemy to fight, or give his name to the enemy, by way of politely introducing himself, before entering into single combat. Popular histories and war stories abound with such examples. A few instances out of many hundreds will suffice to serve as specimens. In the famous battle of the Uji River, Sasaki Takatsuna led the van and crossed the River in the face of the enemy, and upon landing on the opposite bank loudly declared his name :—" I, who lead the van and have crossed the Uji River, am Sasaki Shirō Takatsuna, fourth son of Sasaki Saburō Hideyoshi, who is an inhabitant of the Province of Ōmi and *descendant of the Emperor Uda in the ninth generation.*" In the Battle of Awazu, Kiso Yoshinaka, on coming upon a hostile force, exclaimed :—" Do I err in taking you for the men of the Ichijō family of Kai ? I am Kiso Yoshinaka of the Minamoto Clan, ' Rising-sun

General,' Samano-kami and Iyono-kami, aged thirty-seven, second son of Tatewaki Senjō Yoshikata, who is the grandson of Rokujō Hangwan Tameyoshi, a descendant in the tenth generation from the Emperor Seiwa. Do not let me die by the hand of a nameless soldier! Come and fight in close combat!" The enemy's chief advanced and replied :—" We, two brothers, are Ichijō-no-Jirō Tadayori and Saburō Kanenobu of the same family, sons of Taketa-no-Tarō Nobuyoshi, who is the grandson of Shinra Saburō Yoshimitsu, third son of Iyo-no-kami Yoriyoshi of the same clan of Minamoto."[1] Thus, it will be seen that they not only declared their own names, but also gave the names of their ancestors. Nay more, even the ghost appears in his ancestral name! In a famous Japanese lyrical drama *Nō* entitled 'Funa Benkei' (Benkei-in-the-ship, 船辨慶) there is a ghost scene, the words of which are in the mouth of every educated Japanese. The scene is so graph-

---

1. The Gempei Seisui Ki, xxxv. (源平盛衰記第三十五卷)

ically described, and the words are so beautifully rendered by Mr. G. B. Sansom, that I am tempted to incur the risk of making a slight digression by quoting his translation at some length. I do so with his kind permission. He first describes the scene thus:—". . . then the boat puts out. A high wind arises, and wraiths of women come clinging to the sides, omens of disaster. Presently a great host of spectres emerge from the waves. They are the ghosts of the men of the Taira clan, drowned in the great sea-fight at Dan-no-ura. The young Emperor is there, the nobles, the generals, the captains, and at their head is Tomomori. *He in a loud voice names himself*, and advances upon Yoshitsune to avenge as a spirit his defeat while in the flesh. Yoshitsune would defend himself with mortal weapons, but Benkei pushes to the front, and by dint of prayer exorcises the unfriendly ghosts. They withdraw, and yet approach again, but, bending to their oars, the boatmen drive the ship on, leave them at last behind, and gain the shore."

Then follows the verse:—

> "Benkei   Ah! Woe is me! The wind has changed....
> Retainer   Musashi Dono, there is a sea spirit clinging to the ship.
> Benkei   Be still! Such things may not be said on shipboard.
> > But lo! How wonderful!
> > Looking over the sea
> > behold arising
> > floating on the waters
> > all the men of Taira
> > that we defeated in the West.
> > Well might they seek
> > this present moment for revenge.
>
> Yoshitsune Ah Benkei.
> Benkei   I stand before thee.
> Yoshitsune There is no cause for fear. What though evil spirits should threaten to wreak vengeance on us, how can aught happen?
> > The whole house of Taira
> > sunk by the will of heaven in the sea for piled-up perfidies and disregard of Gods' and Buddhas' holy grace.
>
> The Chorus First his High Majesty
> > and the moon-nobles
> > and the cloud-guests
> > like mists on the mountains
> > have appeared floating
> > over the waves.
>
> Tomomori's Ghost *This is I,*
> > *Offspring of the Emperor Kwammu*
> > *in the ninth generation,*

Taira no Tomomori
his ghost!

    Lo! Yoshitsune, 'tis thou! Strangely met!
The Chorus Just as Tomomori sank,
    So he would overwhelm
    Yoshitsune in the waves,
    the floating waves
    around him his long halberd
    in circles like the tomoe,
    splashing in the tide,
    breathing vile vapours.
    Their eyes grow dizzy
    their breasts perturbed
    their senses gone almost.
Yoshitsune Then Yoshitsune, all undismayed,
    then Yoshitsune, all undismayed,
    drawing his weapon
    and as one facing
    a living foeman
    would with him strive.
    But Benkei arising
    thrusts him aside
    and as he cries
    Here will sword-work nought avail!
    grasping his rosary
    rattles the beads between his palms...."[1]

We now pass to the ceremonies of the Buddhists. Their offerings usually consist of tea,

---

1. G. B. Sansom, *Translation from Lyrical Drama*: "*Nō*," in the Transactions of the Asiatic Society of Japan, vol. XXXVIII, part iii. 1911.

rice, fruits, cakes and flowers, either artificial or natural, the most usual being lotus. Fish and meat form no part of the sacrifice, because of the doctrine of abstinence from flesh, embodied in Buddha's commandment not to kill any animate being. Whether the ceremony takes place in a temple or in a home, priests officiate and recite sacred books. When it is performed in a temple, sacred music generally accompanies the prayer-recitals. The assembly in turn burn incense and prostrate themselves before the altar, the order of precedence being the same as in the case of Shintō worship. The feast, which is held in the house on the preceding evening, does not differ in its general features from that of the Shintōists, except that the food consists of vegetables only.

In addition to the ceremonies performed on the three occasions referred to, there are *three appointed times* in the course of a year, when people offer sacrifices to the spirits of ancestors, both at home and at the graves. These are *Higan* ("the other shore" 彼岸), or the spring

THE WORSHIP OF FAMILY-ANCESTORS 65

and autumn Equinoctial Festivals of the dead, who are supposed to cross the ocean of existence and reach *the other shore*, that is Nirvana; and *Urabon*, or the *Bon* Festival, which continues from the 13th till the 16th of July. In *Higan* the family graves are visited, and flowers and water offered upon the tombs. In *Urabon* the festival for the "Invitation of Spirits" is held in every Buddhist's house. On the day previous to the *Bon* Festival, markets called *Kusa-ichi* or *Bon-ichi* are held in many places for the sale of articles used in the decoration of altars. On the 14th of July, visits to the family graves and offerings of flowers and lanterns are made, and shelves are erected in the houses called *shōryō-dana* (精靈棚), or "the shelf for the spirits," which are decorated with various kinds of vegetables and large lanterns called *kiriko-dōro*. On the evening of the 13th, the *mukai-bi*, or "reception fire," is kindled before the door of the house or in the garden; and on the evening of the 16th, *okuri-bi*, or the "farewell fire," is lighted. During these four days, the spirits are supposed to come and stay in the house. Priests are invited to recite prayers, and many offerings of rice, water, fruits, cakes and vegetables are made on the "spirit-shelf," the most curious among the offerings being oxen made of fruits of the egg-plant and horses fashioned from white melons, the legs being represented by hemp-stalks. Elaborate rules regulate the nature of the offerings of this festival, but it is unnecessary to dwell upon them here.

The extent of the sacrifices made on the occasion of the periodical services, which I have described, and the number of priests, who perform the ceremony, as well as the size and decorations of the ancestral graves, vary in accordance with the rank and fortune of the people. One of the most magnificent edifices in Japan is the temple of Nikkō, which is dedicated to the worship of Iyeyasu, first Shōgun of the Tokugawa family. There is a well-known popular saying "Never say *kekkō* (splendid)

SHINTŌ OFFERINGS BEFORE THE TOMB

THE WORSHIP OF FAMILY-ANCESTORS 67

until you see Nikkō." In the early part of the Tokugawa Shōgunate, one thousand priests took part in the ceremonies of worship on the occasions of *nenki* of the ancestors of Shōgun, and recited one thousand sacred books every day, until they had completed the recitation of ten thousand volumes in ten days. Of course, these festivals, which sometimes took place two or three times a year, entailed great expense on the treasury of the State, and also on the feudal nobles, who were compelled to make contributions of rice and money. At the beginning of the 18th century, however, a new law was enacted, by which the number of priests was limited to two or three hundred, the number of the sacred books to be recited to one thousand volumes and the duration of the festival to three or four days. This reform is said to have reduced the expense to one-tenth of the original amount. This fact demonstrates the importance attached to the worship of ancestors.

The worship of ancestors is not limited only

to the festival times mentioned. When a young student goes to Europe or America to pursue his studies, when a soldier sets out on a campaign, when an official is sent abroad on some government mission, or when a merchant undertakes a long journey on business, he invariably visits the graves of his ancestors in order to take leave of them. When they live in places distant from their ancestral graves, they very often make long journeys in order to visit the tombs and make sacrifices to them. In many Shintōists' houses, the offerings of saké and *sakaki*-tree are continually made; and in Buddhists' houses flowers are offered every day and incense is continually burnt on the *Butsudan*. In fact, the worship of the spirits of ancestors forms part of the everyday life of the people.

Shintō Offerings before the Coffin

PART III

ANCESTOR-WORSHIP AND LAW

ANCESTOR-WORSHIP AND LAW

CHAPTER I

The Government

I have been at some pains to describe the present state of Ancestor-worship in Japan, in order to show that even now the social life of the people is greatly influenced by the practice. Now I come to the main subject of this paper; namely, the relation of Ancestor-worship to Japanese Law.

That the foundation of our government was the worship of ancestors is shown by the word for government, *matsuri-goto*, which literally signifies "affairs of worship." The ceremony of *Seiji-hajime* (政事始), or the "Commencement of the Affairs of State," which takes place on the 4th of January, consists in the Emperor receiving from his Ministers the report of the affairs of the Great Shrine at Isé. (先奏伊勢神宮之事). Thus, the business of our government may be said to begin every year with matters relating to worship. "*Sai-sei Itchi*" (祭政一致), or "the unity of worship and government" is an expression, which was very commonly used by old writers on politics and government. Upon this principle, even after the introduction of Chinese civilization in ancient times and the great reform of the Taikwa Era (大化) (645–649 A. D.), the *Jingi Kwan* (神祇官), or the "Department of Divine Worship" was given precedence over all other government departments, even over the Dajō Gwan (太政官), or the "Great Council of State," which latter controlled things temporal.

The most minute regulations with respect to rituals of worship are to be found in the old law-books, such as the Taihō Code (大寶令) and the Yengi Shiki (延喜式); and all great affairs of State, such as the promulgation of the Constitution, the declaration of war, the conclusion of peace, and the revision of treaties with foreign powers, are reported to the Great Shrine of the First Imperial Ancestor at Isé, and sometimes also to the graves of other Imperial Ancestors.

Immediately after the conclusion of war with Russia, Meiji Tennō proceeded to the Great Shrine at Isé to conduct the thanks-giving ceremonies in person. Taishō Tennō, then the Crown Prince, also visited Isé soon after His August Father, and paid homage to the Great Shrine, Admiral Tōgō, on his triumphal return from his great victory in the Battle of the Japan Sea, immediately proceeded to the Isé Bay with his fleet, and paid a visit to the Great Shrine, with the Commanders of the Squadrons, their staffs and the Captains of the warships, leading three battalions of marines with arms and a thousand men without arms, and there the ceremony of thanksgiving was held on the 18th of October 1905. The late Prince Itō, on being appointed Resident-General of Corea, also went to Isé to pay his respect to the Great Shrine, before setting out for his new post in the Protectorate.

High officials, sent abroad on duty or returning from it, are ordered to worship at the Temple of the First Imperial Ancestor in the Sanctuary of the Imperial Palace, after they are given audience by His Majesty the Emperor.

Thus, in Japan, as it was in China, "the great affairs of State are Worship and War." (國之大事在祀與戎).[1]

---

1. 左傳, *Commentaries of Sa on the Spring and Autumn History of Confucius.*

CHAPTER II

THE CONSTITUTION

The Constitution of the Empire of Japan was promulgated by Meiji Tennō on the 11th of February 1889, that day being the National Festival of *Kigensetsu*, or the anniversary of the foundation of the Empire by the First Emperor Jimmu Tennō. In the framing of this Constitution, Prince Hirobumi Itō (then Count) (伊藤博文), with many high officials, was first sent to Europe with the Imperial commission to examine the constitutions of Western countries, and the principles which find a place in the component elements of constitutional governments have been mostly adopted, so far as they are consistent with the fundamental principle of the form of the Imperial Government, which existed from the beginning of the Empire. That fundamental principle is clearly stated in the 1st Article of the Constitution: " The Empire of Japan shall be reigned over and governed by *a line of Emperors unbroken for ages eternal.*" Prince Itō, in his " Commentaries on the Constitution " (憲法義解, translated into English by Viscount Miyoji Itō 伊東巳代治), says :—" The Sacred Throne of Japan is *inherited from Imperial Ancestors,* and is to be bequeathed to posterity ; in it resides the power to reign over and govern the State." From this it will be seen that the foundation of the Constitution is the worship of the Imperial Ancestors, a fact which is definitely set forth in the Preamble of the Constitution which runs thus :—

" *Having, by virtue of the glories of Our Ancestors, ascended the throne of a lineal succession unbroken for ages eternal ; remembering that Our beloved subjects are the very same that have been favoured with the benevolent care and affectionate vigilance of Our Ancestors,* and desiring to promote their welfare and give development to their moral and intellectual faculties ; and hoping to maintain the prosperity and progress of the State, in concert with Our people and with their support, We hereby promulgate, ... a fundamental law of State, to exhibit the principles, by which We are to be guided in Our conduct, and to point out to what Our descendants and Our subjects and their descendants are forever to conform.

"*The rights of sovereignty of the State, We have inherited from Our Ancestors*, and We shall bequeath them to Our descendants. Neither We nor they shall in future fail to wield them, in accordance with the provisions of the Constitution hereby granted."

The Imperial Speech made on the occasion of the promulgation of the Constitution, also shows that the worship of the Imperial Ancestors is the foundation of the Constitution. His Majesty said :—

"Whereas We make it the joy and glory of Our heart to behold the prosperity of Our country, and the welfare of Our subjects, We do hereby, in virtue of *the supreme power we inherit from Our Imperial Ancestors*, promulgate the present immutable fundamental law, for the sake of Our present subjects and their descendants.

"The *Imperial Founder of Our House and Our other Imperial Ancestors, by the help and support of the forefathers of Our subjects, laid the foundation of Our Empire* upon a basis, which is to last forever. That this brilliant achievement embellishes the annals of Our country, is due to the glorious virtues of Our Sacred Imperial Ancestors, and to the loyalty and bravery of Our subjects, their love of their country and their public spirit. Considering that *Our subjects are the descendants of the loyal and good subjects of Our Imperial Ancestors*, We doubt not but that Our subjects will be guided by Our views, and will sympathize with all Our endeavours, and that, harmoniously co-operating together, they will share with Us Our hope of making manifest the glory of Our country, both at home and abroad, and of securing forever the stability of the work *bequeathed to Us by Our Imperial Ancestors*."

His Majesty further took an oath to the Imperial Ancestors at the Sanctuary of the Palace, to observe the provisions of the Fundamental Law in the following terms :—

"*We, the Successor to the prosperous Throne of Our Predecessors, do humbly and solemnly swear to the Imperial Founder of Our House and to Our other Imperial Ancestors* that, in pursuance of a great policy co-extensive with the Heavens and with the Earth, We shall maintain and secure from decline the ancient form of government.

"In consideration of the progressive tendency of the course of human affairs and in parallel with the advance of civilization, We deem it expedient, in order to give clearness and distinctness to *the instructions bequeathed by the Imperial Founder of Our House and by Our other Imperial Ancestors*, to establish fundamental laws formulated into express provisions of law, so that, on the one hand, Our Imperial posterity may possess an express guide for the course they are to follow, and that, on the other, Our subjects shall thereby be enabled to enjoy a wider range of action in giving Us their support, and that the observance of Our laws shall continue to the remotest ages of time. We will thereby to give greater firmness to the stability of Our country and to promote the welfare of all the people within the boundaries of Our dominions; and We now establish the Imperial House Law and the Constitution. These Laws come to only an exposition of grand precepts for the conduct of the government, *bequeathed by the Imperial Founder of Our House and by Our other Imperial Ancestors.* That We have been so fortunate in Our reign, in keeping with the tendency of the times, as to accomplish this work, *We owe to the glorious Spirits of the Imperial Founder of Our House and of Our other Imperial Ancestors.*

"We now reverently make Our prayer to Them and to Our Illustrious Father, and implore the help of Their Sacred Spirits, and make to Them solemn oath never at this time nor in the future to fail to be an example to Our subjects

THE CONSTITUTION

in the observance of the Laws hereby established.

"May the Heavenly Spirits witness this Our solemn Oath."

The Preamble of the Imperial House Law, which was promulgated on the same day with the Constitution, that is, *Kigensetsu*, or the Festival of the Accession of the First Emperor and the Foundation of the Empire, also shows that the Sovereign Power is the sacred inheritance from the Imperial Ancestors. The terms of the Preamble are the following :—

"The Imperial Throne of Japan, enjoying the Grace of Heaven and everlasting from ages eternal in an unbroken line of succession, has been transmitted to Us through successive reigns. *The fundamental rules of Our Family were established once for all, at the time that Our Ancestors laid foundations of the Empire*, and are even at this day as bright as the celestial luminaries. We now desire *to make the instructions of Our Ancestors more exact and express* and to establish for Our posterity a House Law, by which Our

House shall be founded in everlasting strength, and its dignity be forever maintained. We hereby, with the advice of Our Privy Council, give Our Sanction to the present Imperial House Law, to serve as a standard by which Our descendants shall be guided."

Again, on the occasion of the promulgation of the Supplements to the Imperial House Law which took place on the *Kigensetsu* of 1907, the Emperor took an oath at the Sanctuary of the Imperial Palace and declared that the Supplements were no other than the exposition of the grand precepts bequeathed by the Imperial Ancestors. The Preamble to the Supplements also sets forth the same fundamental principle.

These solemn utterances of the Emperor leave no room for any doubt that the promulgation of the Constitution was in no sense an innovation, but the confirmation of the fundamental principle established by the Imperial Ancestors, that the Throne is the sacred inheritance from the Imperial Ancestors, and the Emperor reigns over and governs the Empire according to the precepts bequeathed by them.

That fundamental principle found expression on the occasion of a recent great event in our history. Meiji Tennō upon receiving the news of the great victory in the Battle of the Japan Sea, was pleased to send the following telegraphic message to Admiral Tōgō and the Combined Fleet under him :—

"Meeting the approaching hostile fleet in the Corean Straits and fighting bravely for days, Our Combined Fleet has achieved an unprecedented success by annihilating the enemy's fleet.

"We are pleased that by your loyalty and bravery, *We have thus been enabled to answer to the Spirits of Our Ancestors.*"

All the newspapers of this country gave graphic descriptions of a striking incident which followed the receipt of the Imperial message. According to the Asahi, all the officers and men under Admiral Tōgō were unable to utter a word, and tears flowed down their sunburnt cheeks in the fullness of their struggling emotions, as the sturdy Admiral read the Imperial message. "For," says the Journal, "'We have thus been enabled to answer to the Spirits of Our Ancestors' are no common words, and there has seldom, if ever, been occasion for these words to leave the Imperial lips."

When Jimmu Tennō founded the Empire, and ascended the throne, the ceremony of coronation consisted in the worship of the Imperial Ancestors on the Hill of Tomi-no-Yama (鳥見山). At the accession of every Emperor there is a ceremony called *Daijō-Sai* (大嘗祭), or *Ōname-no-Matsuri*, usually on the first Festival Day of Shinshō-Sai already referred to, on which the newly crowned Emperor offers the first-fruits of the year to his Ancestors. Article 11 of the Imperial House Law says:— "The ceremonies of Coronation shall be performed and *Daijō-Sai* shall be held at Kyōto." Article 10 of the same Law provides that upon the demise of the Emperor, the Imperial heir shall ascend the Throne, and shall *acquire the Divine Treasures of the Imperial Ancestors*. These Divine Treasures consist of the Mirror before mentioned, a Sword and a Jewel, which have been bequeathed by the First Imperial Ancestor, Amaterasu Ō-Mikami, to her descendants as symbols of the Imperial power.

The foregoing statements lead us to a very peculiar conclusion as to the nature of the government, which may at first sight seem paradoxical, and yet is true. The Emperor holds the sovereign power, not as his own inherent right, but as an inheritance from his Divine Ancestor. The government is, therefore, *theocratical*. The Emperor rules over the country as the supreme head of the vast family of the Japanese nation. The government is, therefore, *patriarchal*. The Emperor exercises the sovereign power according to the Constitution, which is based on the most advanced principles of modern constitutionalism. The government is, therefore, *constitutional*. In other words, the fundamental principle of the Japanese government is *theocratico-patriarchal constitutionalism*. This tripartite character of the government presents the curious meeting of the Past and Present, to which I referred at the outset of this work.

What is it that has brought about this singular form of government? I think the principal causes are two: namely, the topographical conditions of the country and the persistent nature of Ancestor-worship. On the one hand, the insular position of the country at the eastern extremity of the Old World, situated as it is at the farthest point in the Northern Hemisphere from the homes of such seafaring nations of the West, as the Spanish, the Portuguese, the Dutch and the English, made it possible for Japan for a long time to remain unknown to the Western countries; and even after it had become known, to remain isolated from the rest of the world until a recent date. Although thus secluded from other countries for many centuries, the country had in the meantime made progress in Oriental civilization, and the people had been so far advanced in their moral and intellectual capacities as to appreciate Occidental civilization and adopt whatever seemed to them worthy of imitation.

On the other hand, the nature of Ancestor-worship, based as it is on the most natural sentiment of filial devotion, and not, as I submit, on the superstitious motive of the dread of the ghost and its propitiation, allowed its practice to remain unchanged through many vicissitudes of the national life, but, at the same time, never standing in the way of the introduction of Western civilization. The rituals accompanying the worship are comparatively simple, and there are not many superstitions necessarily connected with it. Shintōism, which is based on Ancestor-worship, has no such set of dogmas, no such moral code, no such sacred books as are usually found in other religions. The natural consequence of such simple form of religion has been that the Japanese people have always been tolerant toward other faiths and institutions, unless they are directly opposed to the national practice of Ancestor-worship. It is easy to understand that Chinese learning and institutions were welcomed and readily adopted in the Middle Ages, because they are based upon the doctrine of ancestral cult. Buddhism, indeed, had met with an opposition at first, on the ground that the Japanese people had no need of worshipping other people's gods, because they had their own. But the Buddhists soon learned to harmonize their teachings with the national practice, not only by receiving the native gods as avatars of ancient Buddhas, but also by adapting their doctrines to Ancestor-worship and establishing elaborate rituals for it. Again, Ancestor-worship was no bar to the introduction and spread of Christianity in the sixteenth century by Francis Xavier and his followers; and it was only when suspicion was aroused as to the existence of ulterior political motives on the part of the foreign propagandists that the persecution began.[1]

On the Restoration of Administration to the Emperor in 1868, Shintōism gained ascendancy over Buddhism, and was installed as the only State religion, and the Department of Divine Worship was established which was given precedence over all other departments of the government, as I have said before. But, at the same time, the resolute intention of the new Imperial government to introduce Western civilization was clearly announced by Meiji Tennō. The first act of His Majesty on ascending the throne was to enunciate the fundamental principles of his government in the form of a solemn oath, which has since been known as "the Five Articles of the Imperial Oath" (五箇條之御誓文). His Majesty declared in this oath, on the 14th of March 1868, as follows :—

1. Deliberative assemblies shall be established and all measures of government shall be

---
1. See Clive Holland's *Old and New Japan*, p. 28.

decided by public opinion.
2. All classes, high and low, shall unite in vigorously carrying out the plan of government.
3. Officials, civil and military, and all common people shall, as far as possible, be allowed to fulfil their just desires, so that there may not be any discontent among them.
4. Uncivilized customs of former times shall be broken through, and everything shall be based upon the just and equitable principles of Nature.
5. Knowledge shall be sought for throughout the world, so that the welfare of the Empire may be promoted.

This oath has been made the basis of our national policy. All the subsequent measures of the Imperial government—especially the establishment of the Constitution—was the realization of the principles thus enunciated.[1] I

---

1. N. Hozumi, *The New Japanese Civil Code*, 1.

can speak from personal knowledge, that the principal care of Prince Itō in preparing the draft of the Constitution by the command of his Sovereign was to reconcile and bring into harmony the traditional character of the government, based on the cult of the Imperial Ancestors, with the most advanced principles of modern constitutionalism. Hence the constitution, which begins by declaring that Japan is reigned over and governed by a line of Emperors *unbroken for ages eternal*, that the Emperor is *sacred and inviolable* and that He is the *head of the Empire*, but which immediately proceeds in the next chapter to secure to the subjects almost every right and liberty, which are enjoyed by the citizens of Western countries.

CHAPTER III

THE IMPERIAL HOUSE

As the Imperial Throne is regarded as a heritage from the Imperial Ancestors, and as the Emperor exercises his sovereign power, not as his own inherent right, but as a right inherited from his Ancestors, it is natural that most important events in the Imperial Household regarding the persons of the Emperor and other members of the Imperial Family should be reported to the Ancestors, and the ceremonies relating there to should be performed before the Ancestral Temple at the Sanctuary of the Palace.

According to the "Ordinance relating to the Family Relations in the Imperial House" (皇室親族令)[1], the Birth and Naming of the Emperor's child must be reported to the Kashiko-Dokoro, the Kwōrei-Den and the Shin-Den; and on the fiftieth day after the birth, the newly born

---

1. Imperial House Ordinance, No. III, 1910.

Imperial Prince or Princess must be taken to the Three Temples above mentioned, in order that he or she may render the first homage to the Imperial Ancestors and other deities (Arts. 39, 40.). The same ceremony is observed with regard to the Birth and Naming of a child of the Crown Prince; but in the case of a child of a Shinnō (Imperial male descendants from Imperial sons to Imperial great-great-grandsons) or Wō (Imperial male descendants from the fifth generation downwards)[1], the Birth and Naming are not reported, and the newly born Prince or Princess is taken to the Three Temples, in order that he or she may worship them (Art. 45.).

Next comes the celebration of the " Majority Ceremony." The " Ordinance relating to the Majority Ceremony in the Imperial House " (皇室成年式令)[2] provides, that on the day of the Emperor's attaining the age of majority, the Majority Ceremony shall be held, and a report

---
1. The Imperial House Law, Art. 31.
2. Imperial House Ordinance, No. IV, 1909.

of it shall be made to the Three Temples, and on the same day, an Imperial Messenger for offering sacrifices shall be sent to the Great Shrine, the Graves of Jimmu Tennō, the late Emperor and the late Empress respectively (Art. 3.). The Ceremony shall be held before the Kashiko-Dokoro, and after the ceremony, the Emperor shall worship the Kwōrei-Den and the Shin-Den (Arts. 4, 5.). The same ceremony is also held before the Kashiko-Dokoro, when the Imperial Heir-apparent or any other male member of the Imperial Family attains majority (Arts. 9, 10, 12.).

The Ceremony of the Marriage of the Emperor is also performed before the Ancestral Temple of the Kashiko-Dokoro. On the day, on which the agreement of the Imperial Marriage is made, a report of it is made to the Three Temples of the Imperial Sanctuary, and, at the same time, an Imperial Messenger for offering sacrifices is sent to the Great Shrine, and to the Graves of Jimmu Tennō, the late Emperor and the late Empress respectively. The celebration of the Imperial Marriage is also reported to the Three Temples on the day on which the ceremony takes place; and when the ceremony is finished the newly married Emperor and Empress worship the Kwōrei-Den and the Shin-Den. After the ceremony, the Emperor and the Empress present themselves to the Great Shrine, and to the respective Graves of Jimmu Tennō, the late Emperor and the late Empress.

The ceremonies of marriage of the Crown Prince and other male members of the Imperial Family are also performed before the Kashiko-Dokoro, and the proceedings are nearly the same as those of the Emperor's marriage, except that a Shinnō or Wō is not required to visit the Great Shrine and the Graves of the late Emperor and the late Empress.

When a Nai-Shinnō (Imperial daughter)[1] or any other female member of the Imperial Family is married to a subject, she must worship the

---

1. The Imperial House Law, Art. 31.

Three Temples before the ceremony is performed.[1]

The Institution of the Imperial Heir-apparent is also reported to the Kashiko-Dokoro, the Kwōrei-Den and the Shin-Den on the day of the ceremony, and, at the same time, an Imperial Messenger for offering sacrifices is sent to the Great Shrine and the Graves of Jimmu Tennō and the late Emperor. The Ceremony of the Institution is held before the Kashiko-Dokoro; and after the ceremony, the Crown Prince and the Crown Princess worship the Three Temples of the Imperial Sanctuary.[2]

From what has been said as to the nature of the Imperial Throne, it will be easily inferred that most minute rules exist as to the Ascension of a new Emperor to the Throne and the Ceremony of Coronation. Article 10 of the Imperial House Law provides that "upon the demise of

---

1. The Imperial House Ordinance, No. III, 1910, Ch. ii.
2. The Ordinance relating to the Institution of the Imperial Heir-apparent (立儲令). The Imperial House Ordinance, No. III, 1909. Art. 3, 4, 6.

the Emperor, the Imperial Heir shall ascend the Throne, and shall acquire the *Divine Treasures of the Imperial Ancestors.*"[1] The Ordinance relating to the Ascension to the Imperial Throne (登極令)[2] provides, among others, that on the Ascension of a new Emperor to the Throne, the Chief Master of Rituals shall be ordered to hold the service of worship at the Kashiko-Dokoro, and, at the same time,.the Ascension shall be reported to the Kwōrei-Den and the Shin-Den (Art. 1.). The same Ordinance further provides, that when the date of Coronation Ceremony and Daijō-Sai[3] is fixed, a report of it shall be made to the Three Temples, and, at the same time, an Imperial Messenger for offering sacrifices shall be despatched to the Great Shrine, the Graves of Jimmu Tennō and the four preceding Emperors (Art. 7.); that, on the day of Coronation which takes place at Kyōto,[4] an Imperial

---

1. See p. 84 f.
2. The Imperial House Ordinance, No. 1, 1909.
3. See p. 84.
4. The Imperial House Law, Art. 11.

Messenger shall be sent to the Kwōrei-Den and the Shin-Den to report the proceedings (Art. 12.); and that, when the Ceremony of Coronation is finished, the Emperor, accompanied by the Empress, shall visit the Great Shrine and the Graves of Jimmu Tennō and four preceding Emperors (Art. 16.).

When Regency is instituted on account of the minority of the Emperor, or for any other cause mentioned in the Imperial House Law,[1] the Regent, on assuming the office, must perform the ceremony of worship at the Kashiko-Dokoro, and also make a report of the assumption at the Kwōrei-Den and the Shin-Den.[2]

By the way, it may be mentioned that Kigen-setsu, or the Festival Day of the Ascension of the First Emperor and the Foundation of the Empire, has always been chosen for the promulgation of all the fundamental laws relating to the Imperial power and the Throne; that is to

---

1. Art. 19.
2. The Ordinance relating to Regency (攝政令). The Imperial House Ordinance, No. 11, 1909, Art. 1.

say, the Constitution and the Imperial House Law were published on the Kigensetsu of 1889, the Supplements to the Imperial House Law on the Kigensetsu of 1907, and all the above-named Imperial House Ordinances, except one, the Ordinance relating to the Family Relations, on the Kigensetsu of 1909. These instances form remarkable exceptions to the usual practice not to publish any laws or ordinances on National Festival Days.

I have said above that there are three forms of Ancestor-worship in Japan, and that the worship of the Imperial Ancestors is the *National worship*. The people worship the Great Shrine, not only because it is dedicated to the Divine Ancestor of their August Sovereign, but because they regard the Imperial Ancestor as the ancestor of the whole nation. The nation is considered as forming *one vast family*, the Imperial House standing at its head as the *Principal Family*, and all the subjects under it as members of houses which stand in the relation of *branch families* to the Imperial House. It is for that reason that the word "ōyake" (おほやけ, 大宅), or "Great House," which is now usually used in the meaning of "public," or sometimes of "government," was formerly very frequently used in the sense of the "Imperial Court" or the "Emperor."[1] It is for the same reason again, as is often stated, that *the Imperial House has no clan or family name*; the clan or family names being appellations used to designate divisions or constituent units of this great nation-family, or "the Great House." As the Emperor is identified with this "Great House," his Ancestor is regarded in one sense as the *Ancestor of the whole nation*. Of course, there is a great number of families, which can not claim their descent directly or indirectly from the Imperial family, as will be shown in the next chapter. But they belong to those families, which were either subjugated by the Imperial

---

1. 和訓栞 (Wakun-no-Shiori), 言海 (Genkai); see also 芳賀矢一著, 國民性十論 (Prof. Haga's *Ten Treatises on the National Character*); 高楠順次郎著, 國民道德ノ根柢 (Prof. Takakusu's *The Basis of the National Morality*).

Ancestors or were naturalized from foreign countries and were given their clan-names from the Emperors, so that they became, as it were, engrafted into the stock of the Yamato nation. The saying of an acute observer on Japan, " The Empire is one great family; the family is a little empire "[1] is not a metaphor, but a literal truth. This identification of the Imperial cult with the national cult, and the superposition of the worship of the Imperial Ancestors over the worship of clan and family ancestors explains the loyalty of the Japanese people to the Emperor and their patriotism towards the country, which seems to have aroused the curiosity of other nations in recent years. Japanese devotion to their ruler and their love of the country are religiously maintained by their national worship; or in other words, they are nothing but filial piety " writ large."

The recent event in China may explain, by way of contrast, what I have said as to the

---
1. Percival Lowell, *The Soul of the Far East*, ch. ii.

character of the worship of the Imperial Ancestors in Japan. It was a source of considerable surprise, not unmixed with sympathetic disappointment, to the Japanese people, that on the fall of the great Manchu Dynasty, no Wên-t'ien-hsiang (文天祥) or Chêng-ch'eng-kung (鄭成功) should have appeared to embellish at least the last page of the history of the old Empire. A few exchanges of shots, a truce, the abdication of the infant Emperor, a new Republic, and the Premier and head of the Imperialists elected President! Such things are almost inconceivable to a Japanese mind. Several theories, more or less plausible, have been advanced in newspapers and magazines; but I think no divergence of opinion can exist as to one point, that is, the *difference of the Imperial cult and the national cult.* In China, the worship of the ancestors of the Manchu Dynasty was the *worship of the Imperial House only*, not the worship of the people, who belong to the Han race. The ancestor of the Imperial House was a conqueror, and the people were the descendants of the conquered. The Imperial House and the people stood in the relation of the conqueror and the conquered; or, in other words, their relations were those of subjugation and submission, and not of reverence and obedience as in the case of Japan. Nearly three hundred years of the Manchu rule does not seem to have produced any change in this irreconcilable relationship between the ruler and the ruled. In Japan, the Emperor is regarded as the head of a vast family, of which the people themselves are members; in China, the Emperor ruled, indeed, but belonged to a race different from that of the people. In Japan, the worship of the Imperial Ancestors is the national cult; in China, it was the cult of the Imperial House only. Can anyone reasonably wonder—though we can not still help wondering to some extent—that the Chinese people should have assumed such an indifferent attitude toward the deplorable fate of the Manchu Dynasty?

CHAPTER IV

THE PEOPLE

I have already stated that the worship of the Imperial Ancestors is our national worship. They are worshipped, not only because they are the ancestors of our August Sovereign, but because they are the Sovereigns of our ancestors. Formerly, as has been stated, the people of Japan was divided into three classes or "Three Bodies" (三體), and each class was divided into many clans. Each individual subject had an *uji*, or clan-name, which was the mark of descent from a certain ancestor. Each clan, whether "great" or "small," had its chief, called *uji-no-kami* (氏上), who was usually the eldest male descendant of the eponymous ancestor. He was obeyed and honoured by the clansmen as the representative of their common ancestor. He was the head of their worship, their leader in time of war, and their governor in time of peace. Small clansmen were governed by the *uji-no-kami* of the small clan, who was himself subject to the *uji-no-kami* of the great clan. During the early epoch in our history known as the " Fujiwara Period," extending over the period of three hundred years (about 670 to 1050 A. D.), when the Fujiwara Clan engrossed the power of the State, and its members held all the great posts of the government, the office of *Kwanpaku*, or Prime Minister, belonged to the *Chōja*, or *uji-no-kami*, of the Fujiwara Clan. It is for the same reason that during the Tokugawa Shōgunate, each Shōgun held the title of *Genji-no-Chōja*, or " the Eldest of the Minamoto Clan."

The Emperor was the supreme authority over them all, and the laws and proclamations of the Imperial Government were transmitted to the *uji-no-kami* of great clans, who, in turn, transmitted them to the *uji-no-kami* of small clans, and thus each clan which was *a body founded on the community of blood and worship, formed an administrative division* of the country, corresponding to the present administrative divisions, such as provinces, cities, towns, districts and villages. Since the great Reform of the Taikwa Era (大化), in spite of the fact that the clan system of government continued for a long time afterward, the basis of the administrative divisions of the country gradually changed from being *personal* to being *territorial*. As Dr. W. E. Hearn very truly remarks, the order of transition "was from kinship to neighbourhood."[1]

The wide and permanent influence, which Ancestor-worship exercises on the national character of the people, may be known from the Imperial Rescript on Education, which was issued by Meiji Tennō on the 30th of October 1890. On that day, the Emperor summoned Prince (then Count) Aritomo Yamagata (山縣有朋), the then Prime Minister and Count (then Mr.) Akimasa Yoshikawa (芳川顯正), the then Minister of Education, and delivered to them the following Rescript :—

---

1. Hearn, *The Aryan Household*, ch. **xvi**.

"Know ye, Our subjects:

"Our *Imperial Ancestors have founded Our Empire on a basis broad and everlasting, and have deeply and firmly implanted virtue*; Our subjects ever united in loyalty and filial piety have from generation to generation illustrated the beauty thereof. This is the glory of the fundamental character of Our Empire, and herein also lies the source of Our education. Ye, Our subjects, be filial to your parents, affectionate to your brothers and sisters; as husbands and wives be harmonious, as friends true; bear yourselves in modesty and moderation; extend your benevolence to all; pursue learning and cultivate arts, and thereby develop intellectual faculties and perfect moral powers; furthermore advance public good and promote common interests; always respect the Constitution and observe the laws; should emergency arise, offer yourselves courageously to the State; and thus guard and maintain the prosperity of Our Imperial Throne coeval with heaven and earth. So shall ye not only be Our good and faithful subjects, but *render illustrious the best traditions of your forefathers.*

"*The Way here set forth is indeed the teaching bequeathed by Our Imperial Ancestors, to be observed alike by Their Descendants and the subjects*, infallible for all ages and true in all places. It is Our wish to lay it to heart in all reverence, in common with you, Our subjects, that we may all attain to the same virtue."[1]

The next day, the Minister of Education caused a copy of the Rescript to be sent to every school in the Empire, with instructions that those engaged in the work of education should bear constantly in mind the spirit of this Imperial Rescript in the discharge of their duties. Now a copy of the Rescript is hung up in every school from universities down to primary schools. It is read and explained to the pupils on ceremonial and other suitable occasions, and every pupil knows it by heart and recites it. In this way,

---

1. The English translation by the Department of Education.

it is now the basis of the moral teaching of the people, and no one who reads it can deny that the foundation of the moral obligation is laid on Ancestor-worship, that is, the reverence which we owe to the Imperial Ancestors, as the "Way" set forth in the Imperial Rescript is the teaching bequeathed by them.

CHAPTER V

THE HOUSE

In the Middle Ages, clans began to gradually disintegrate, and households took their place. It was only after the Restoration of 1868, that the house-system began to lose its force and that the individual, not the household, began to form the unit of the State. This transition may be illustrated by the history of our *Law of Registration*. The development of this law may be divided into *three epochs*: (1) the Epoch of *Clan-registration* (姓氏錄時代); (2) the Epoch of *House-registration* (戶籍時代); and (3) the Epoch of *Personal registration* (身分登記時代). In those early days, when the clan formed the unit of the State, it was of the utmost importance that each person's clan-name should be kept sacred. As only those who belonged to certain clans could fill high official positions or join the Imperial body-guard, and as several other privileges were enjoyed by particular clans, attempts were often made to forsake original clans and surreptitiously adopt the names of some other influential clans. In order to put a stop to these abuses, an "ordeal of hot water" or *kugadachi* (探湯) was held in obedience to an Imperial Proclamation in the fourth year of the Emperor Inkyō (允恭天皇) (415 A. D.) to test the truth or falsehood of the clan-names borne by the people. This ordeal consisted in plunging the hand into hot water before the temple of a god, and it was claimed that those who had assumed false clan-names would suffer injury, whilst the innocent would escape unhurt. In the fifth year of the Era of Tempyō Hōji (天平寶字) (761 A. D.), an office called Sen-Shizokushi-Jo (撰氏族志所) was founded for the compilation of a clan-registry, and a commission was appointed which numbered amongst its members the most distinguished scholars of the time. The work of the commission was, however, not completed. Since that time, Imperial proclamations were frequently issued ordering all clans in the Empire to send their genealogical records (本系帳) to the government, in order that they might be included in the Imperial archives. It was ordered, that in those records, the name of the first ancestor and also the name of the ancestor from whom the small clan branched out, should always be given, and the records of those claiming to belong to noble clans had to be attested by the head of the whole clan with his signature. In the reign of the Emperor Saga (嵯峨天皇), in the sixth year of the Kōnin Era (弘仁) (815 A. D.), "the Register of Clan-names," or "Shōji Roku" (姓氏錄), was compiled, a part of which is still in existence to-day. This Register consisted of thirty volumes, and contained 1,182 clan-names. In that year, Kan-kei-Jo (勘系所), or the Bureau of Genealogical Investigation, was established. The preservation of genealogical records and their accuracy were considered to be matters of the utmost importance in those times. and their loss or forgery used to supply abundant material to the writers of novels and dramas, just as the loss or forgery of wills is frequently made the subject of fiction by Western writers.

The introduction of *ko-seki* (戸籍), House-registry, dates back as far as 645 A. D., the first year of the Taikwa Era, when great reforms were made in the system of government. Although its introduction was earlier in date than the final compilation of the "Register of Clan-names," its historical order must come after that of the Clan-registry, for the system of House-registry has continued from that remote period down to the present time.

It was only in the 31st Year of Meiji (1898) that the history of our law of registration began to enter upon the third stage of the development. The present law, which was promulgated in 1898, and which replaced the previous law of 1871, still retains the name of *Koseki Hō* (戸籍法), or "the Law of House-Registration," but the character of the law has undergone a change, necessitated by the progress of the social condition of the country, for it provides for the registration of *individual status*, or *mibun-tōki* (身分登記), as well as for house-registration.[1]

It is often asserted by writers, who concern themselves with the early phenomena of society, that a family was the original unit of the State, and that the aggregation of families formed a clan. But this view seems to me to reverse the real order of development. It was the clan which was first recognized by law, and which formed the unit of society. The family was included in the clan, but did not yet possess separate existence in the eye of the law. It was only by the gradual disintegration of the clan, that the family or house came to the fore, and began to form the unit of society. Thus, the constituent element of society becomes smaller and smaller, until it divides itself into an atom or individual.

---

1. This system of the registration of individual status was abolished in 1915 for the sole reason that it is most inconvenient to keep separate official books for the two kinds of registration.

From what has been stated relating to the development of the law of registration, it will be seen that Japan is now in a state of transition. Until recently, a house was a corporation and a legal unit of the State. But ever since the Restoration of 1868, the family system has gradually decayed, until, at present, the house has entirely lost its corporate character. Formerly, it was the head of the family only, who could fill an official position, serve in the army, and hold property. But as a result of a reform in the system of government, the house-members were permitted to fill public positions, and with the reform of the law of military conscription, both the house-head and the house-members began to be liable to military duties; while with the progress of commerce and industry, the house-members came to be entitled to hold public bonds, stocks and shares, which the law now recognizes as their separate property. Although the house has thus lost its corporate existence in the eye of the law, nevertheless it still retains its character as the unit of society. The new Civil Code, which came into operation in 1898, allows a house-member, who is not a legal heir presumptive to the house-headship, to secede from a household and establish a new "branch-house" with the consent of the head of the family (Art. 743, 744); for the law recognizes the tendency of social progress towards individualism, but, at the same time, it makes careful provisions for the continuity of the house. The *house is the seat of Ancestor-worship*, and, therefore, the discontinuance of the house implies the discontinuance of its cult. It is for that reason that the Civil Code contains many strict rules against the discontinuance of the house. Article 762 provides:—

"A person who has established a *new house* may abolish it and enter another house.

"A person who has become the head of a house *by succession cannot abolish such a house*, except where permission to do so has been obtained from a court of law for the purpose of succession to, or the re-establishment of, the main house, or for any other just cause."

If we compare the first with the second clause of the article above cited, we at once see that this provision is made for the purpose of the continuance of Ancestor-worship. Those who establish new houses *have no house-ancestor to worship* and therefore they are at liberty, if so disposed, to abolish such houses, and to become members of other houses by adoption, marriage or any other arrangement. But with those who have *succeeded* to a house-headship, the case is different. They are entrusted with the duty of the worship, which it is considered the greatest act of impiety to discontinue. But if they belong to *branch* houses, they may abolish them in order to continue or revive the worship of the *ancestors of the main house*, from which their own have sprung.

For the same reason, it is provided in Article 744 that "the legal presumptive heir to the headship of a house is not permitted to enter another house, or establish a new one, except in cases where the necessity arises for succeeding to the headship of the main house." A legal presumptive heir is *heres necessarius*, and to him falls the duty of succeeding to the headship of his house and of upholding the continuity of the worship of its ancestors. For that reason, he or she cannot become a member of another house by marriage, adoption or by any other cause, nor found a house of his or her own, except where the more important duty of preserving the continuity of the worship of the ancestors of the main house renders such a step necessary. Sometimes hardships arise from the operation of this rule. For instance, a male head of a household or a male legal presumptive heir of a house cannot marry the only daughter of the head of another house, owing to the fact that she is the legal presumptive heiress to the headship of the latter house. In such cases, the only alternative is to disinherit the heiress according to the provision of the Code, which requires the judgment of a court of law (Art. 975), and thus enable her to enter another house by marriage.

In recent years, it has become very common for noble and rich families to establish house-laws in order to regulate their household affairs, especially with regard to the family and property relations. The Peerage Ordinance of 1907 (華族令) allows the Peers to establish house-laws, with the sanction of the Minister of the Imperial Household.[1] The house-laws of aristocratic or rich families, whether established under this Ordinance or otherwise, have a common feature which shows that their foundation is laid almost without exception on Ancestor-worship. The house-law usually begins with a preamble, reciting that it is established in accordance with the instructions bequeathed by the ancestors, or that it is established in order to put the ancestral house on a firm basis. At the beginning of the house-law, an article is almost invariably found, enjoining the head and members of the house

---
1. The Imperial House Ordinance, No. 11, 1907.

to observe the duty of the worship of the house-ancestors. At the end, the oath by members of the house is usually affixed, that they will faithfully observe the provisions of the house-law.

Let me take as a specimen the house-law of a certain Count's house, and translate a portion of it, in order to show the fundamental character of the house-laws.

"THE PREAMBLE:—I, A. B., in spite of my unworthiness, have the honour of being ranked in the Peerage by the Gracious Favour of the Emperor, which *was accorded to our Ancestor* on account of the distinguished service which he had rendered to his sovereign and country. Since I succeeded to this honourable position a thought has never left my mind that I have assumed a heavy responsibility of following the *instructions bequeathed by our Ancestors*, by supporting the dignity of the Imperial House above, and by maintaining the prestige and prosperity of our House below, thereby requiting the Gracious Imperial Favours which were accorded to our House. To fulfil this responsibility, I have hereby established eighty-six articles of our House Law, and exhibit the principles by which we and our descendants are to be guided. I hereby reverently *report the establishment of this fundamental law of our family to the Spirits of our Ancestors, and swear to them* that I shall set an example to my descendants by faithfully observing its provisions. I command my present and future descendants to observe most strictly the provisions of this House Law, and never to swerve from the *course of duty prescribed by their ancestors.*

CHAPTER I General Rules

Art. 1. The head and members of this House shall be loyal to the Imperial House, shall obey the laws of the State, and shall never behave in such a way as to disgrace the prestige of the Peerage.

Art. 2. *The worship of the Ancestors of the*

House shall be specially attended to, and the glory of the Ancestors shall be maintained.

Art. 3. Intimate and harmonious connections shall be kept up among relatives of the blood and relatives of the House; just and upright conduct shall be maintained, and education of house-members shall be encouraged, so that the prosperity of the house shall continue forever.

CHAPTER II The House-head

Art. 4. The house-head shall administer the house according to the provisions of this House Law.

Art. 5. The wife of the house-head and of his heir-apparent shall be selected from among the Peers.

*   *   *   *   *

Art. 12. Each house-member, on his or her attaining the age of majority, or one who becomes a house-member by marriage, adoption or otherwise, on his or her entering the House, *shall take oath before the Spirits of the House Ancestors* to observe the provisions of this House Law.

* * * * *

" We, the undersigned, recognizing that the above House Law is established for the purpose of maintaining the prosperity of our House and of promoting the welfare of its members, by securing forever the stability of the *work bequeathed by our Ancestors* and by laying the foundation of the House on a firm basis, reverently *take oath before the Spirits of our Ancestors*, that we shall strictly follow its rules and never in future attempt to change its provisions without a sufficient cause.

(Signed and sealed) A. C.

A. D.

* *"

CHAPTER VI

Marriage

Marriage is an institution based upon human nature; but the original cause of its recognition by law must be sought for in Ancestor-worship. The Li Chi or "The Book of Rituals" (禮記) defines marriage as the "union of the affection of two persons bearing different clan-names, for the purpose of *serving the ancestral mausoleum* on the one hand, and of *continuing future generations* on the other." (婚禮者將合二姓之好,上以事宗廟而下以禮後世也)[1] This old Chinese definition exactly tallies with the primitive notion of marriage.

The State recognized wedlock, and began to make rules for its protection, because it was regarded as a *means of perpetuating the worship of ancestors*. In the eye of the old law, it was essential that a family should perpetuate itself for

---

1. 昏義

ever, and marriage represented the union of man and woman for the purpose of obtaining a successor to maintain the continuity of Ancestor-worship. It was due to the dead that the descendants should not become extinct. Marriage was therefore a means to an end, and that end was the continuity of the family cult. It was considered one of the greatest misfortunes that could befall a man, to die without leaving a son to perpetuate the worship of his ancestors and himself. Mencius (孟子) says:—"There are three things which are unfilial, and to have no posterity is the greatest of them." (不孝有三無後爲大) In passing, it may be noted that the other two unfilial things are encouraging parents in unrighteousness, and not succouring parents in poverty and old age. To be without posterity by not marrying is a greater fault than the other two, because it is *an offence against the whole line of ancestors*, and terminates the sacrifice to them. In the "Book of Filial Piety" (孝經) Confucius says:—"There are three thousand acts which are punished by the Five Punishments, but no crime is greater than filial impiety." (五刑之屬三千而罪莫大於不孝) If impiety is the greatest crime, and if the failure to have posterity is the greatest impiety, there can be no greater crime that a man can commit than to remain single. The reason of this doctrine of Chinese moral philosophy, which has been taught in our country for more than one thousand years, is obvious. It was believed that the posthumous happiness of the ancestors of a family depended on the proper performance of the family cult. It was, therefore, the *duty* of every head of a house to marry for the purpose of avoiding the calamity of the family cult becoming extinct.

It was the established principle of our customary law, which is maintained with some modifications in the new Civil Code (Art. 750), that *a member of a house must obtain the consent of the head of the family* for his or her marriage. The House Law, or "Ko-ryō" (戶令), of the Taihō Code also required the consent of grandparents, parents and other relatives before a marriage could be celebrated. According to Article 750 of the new Civil Code, if a member of a house marries without the consent of the head of the family, the latter may, within one year from the day of the marriage, exclude him or her from the household, or, if he or she has entered another house by marriage, forbid his or her return to the original house in case of dissolution of the marriage. As to the consent of parents, the first clause of Article 772 provides:—" For contracting a marriage, a child must obtain the consent of the parents, who are *in the same house*. But this rule does not apply if man has completed his thirtieth year or woman her twenty-fifth year." The consequences of a marriage without the consent of the parents are stated in Articles 783 and 784. The parent may make application to a court of law for the annulment of the marriage within a period of six months from the time when he or she first became acquainted with the fact of the marriage, or within two years from the date of its registration.

The reason for requiring the consent of the head of the family is, that by the marriage of a male member, another member is added to the household; or in the case of marriage of a female member, one member is lost to it, for the wife enters the house of her husband, unless a man marries a female house-head, or an adopted son marries a "house-daughter," or the daughter of an adopter, in which cases the husband enters the house of his wife according to the provision of Article 788. In all cases, marriage brings about a change in the household, and this is the reason assigned at present for the existence of the rule relating to the permission of the heads of families.

But formerly, there was another, and no doubt *more important*, reason. As marriage was regarded *as the means of obtaining a successor to the sacra of the house*, it was incumbent upon the house-head to guard against any improper alliance.

The consent of the parents in the same house

is also required by the new Civil Code, chiefly because the parents, who have the interest of their children at heart, may be relied upon to proffer good advice and to guard against any rash or unsuitable union; and also because of the reverence which is due to them from the children. But here, as in the case of the consent of the house-head, the original cause of the rule is different from the reason of its retention. At first, the parent's consent was required, because a son's marriage was the means of obtaining a successor to continue his *sacra*; and in the case of a daughter, she passed out of the original household, and was initiated into the cult of her husband's house. That it was the supreme duty of a man to marry for the purpose of obtaining the continuator of the family cult may be gathered from the Dialogue of Mencius (孟子). A famous Chinese Emperor Shun (舜), who was noted for his filial piety, married without obtaining the consent of his parents, for he knew that they would not countenance

any union, and he could not marry if he had asked for their consent. Mencius, in justifying the act, said:—" Shun married without informing his parents because of his anxiety lest he should have no posterity. Superior men consider that his action under the circumstances should be regarded as if he had informed them."
(舜不告而娶爲無後也君子以爲猶告也)

Although Chinese laws and philosophy were introduced into Japan in ancient times, the famous Chinese law prohibiting *marriage between persons bearing the same clan-name* (同姓不娶) was not followed in our old Codes. The reason of this remarkable deviation from the ordinary course seems to be this: an ancestor only *receives the sacra of his blood descendants* (異姓不祭) and a marriage between persons belonging to the same clan—that is, between persons descended from the same ancestor—was, perhaps, rather to be favoured than an alliance with a person of another clan, for the issue of the marriage would be of the unmixed blood of the ancestor. This exception to the general adoption of the Chinese laws appears the more remarkable, by reason of the fact that the prohibition against the adoption of a child from a different clan, which has existed and still exists in Chinese law, was included in our old Codes, almost without any modification.

The consequence of the doctrine above stated is that, although celibacy was not positively forbidden by law, it was denounced by public opinion, which is often as strong as, or even stronger than, law. In fact, the obligation to marry was so effectively insisted upon by opinion, that there was no need of enforcing it by legislation. In the "Hundred Articles of Tokugawa," which is commonly known among foreigners as the "Legacy of Iyeyasu," there is, indeed, one article which prohibits celibacy declaring that "no one should remain single after sixteen years of age, for it is the great law of morality based on human nature that man and woman should marry." But this article is found only in one manuscript text, and not in others, especially in one which was found at the Shōgun's Archives. Whatever may be said of the authenticity of the text, the existence of this rule does not much affect the weight of the above statement, as the "Hundred Articles" was part of the secret laws of the Shōgunate and was not published to the people—all the more so, as certain members of family were not allowed to obey this "great law of morality based on human nature." It must be noticed that this customary prohibition of celibacy only extended to the *present or future head of a family*. As to the other members of family, on the contrary, celibacy was, as a rule, obligatory. This rule which existed before the Restoration of 1868 clearly shows in what light marriage was regarded by our old law. Formerly, only the house-head, his eldest son who was the presumptive heir and his eldest grandson who would become the presumptive heir after the eldest son, was allowed—or obliged—to marry, but younger sons could not lawfully contract marriage. There was no need for the latter to marry and have children, because they had no apparent hope of ever becoming house-heads, and continuators of the cult. This rule was strictly followed among *samurai*, or military class, for permission was not given by their feudal lords for the marriage of younger sons. Among merchants, artisans and farmers, there were sometimes exceptional cases in certain localities, but in such cases, the newly married couple generally established a " new house."

The legal recognition of concubinage also found its justification in the paramount importance of having an issue to perpetuate ancestral cult. There is no doubt that concubinage took its rise in the licentiousness of a powerful class among the people. Chiefs and warriors had more power of securing women, either by capturing them from other tribes or wresting them from men of their own tribe. Later, when rudimentary commerce began, rich men also bought many women for their wives. As the possession of many women implied courage, wisdom, wealth or noble descent on the part of the possessor, plurality of wives naturally came to be regarded as a mark of social distinction. But, on the other hand, the majority of common people were compelled to content themselves with one wife, chiefly on account of their economic conditions. Even among the upper classes, distinctions began to be made among a man's wives, on account of such causes as favouritism by the husband, the social position of the family of the wife's birth, the order of giving birth to a male child and the like. Thus, in the course of time, the custom grew up of recognizing one of them as the chief or legitimate wife, and all others as wives of inferior grade or concubines.

When monogamy became the rule and came to be generally approved, necessity arose for inventing a reason for maintaining the institution of concubinage. The powerful class did not like to acknowledge openly that their mistresses were kept simply for the gratification of their licentious desire. And the reason was not far to seek in an ancestor-worshipping society. Among them, the paramount importance of perpetuating the cult was thought to justify almost everything. It was alleged that concubines were kept in order to provide against the much dreaded misfortune of the extinction of the cult by the failure of issue. When there was no child or no male offspring, it was considered that the fault lay with the wife, so that she could be divorced, and a new wife taken, or a concubine might be kept, in order to raise the issue. It was further ingeniously asserted that nobles and men of rank could keep a number of concubines, because of the greater importance of maintaining their family cult. Hence, the greater the importance of the family, the greater the number of concubines. These allegations were, as might be easily suspected, in most cases, nothing more than a pretext—or, rather, it may be more correct to say that the reason was often misapplied and made a pretext. If the real cause of permitting concubinage was to get a successor to the family cult, it could only be permitted in case of the failure of male offspring by the legitimate wife. Moreover, the prevalence of the custom of adopting a son to succeed to the family worship made the recourse to this institution practically unnecessary. But, under the old regime, it was usual for the noble families to keep concubines notwithstanding that they had children by their legitimate wives. But, for this again, it was said that the upper classes needed more than one child to meet the possible contingency of the failure of an heir by the death of the only child, or by successive deaths of many children—the more the better, because the more secure.

For reasons such as above stated, the old Taihō Code (701 A. D.) recognized concubinage and gave the concubine the status of the second rank in the family relationship. The Criminal Code of 1870 followed the Taihō Code, but concubinage was abolished with the promulgation of the Criminal Code of 1880. Although the new Civil Code lays great importance on Ancestor-worship, it does not recognize the institution of concubinage, as it is not only immoral, but unnecessary for the maintenance of the family cult, which may be provided for in many other ways. It is clear that concubinage did not take its rise in Ancestor-worship. Here, as in many other cases, the fact existed, and the reason followed.

CHAPTER VII

Divorce

In the House Law (Ko-ryō) of the Taihō Code are enumerated the famous Seven Grounds of Divorce (七出之狀). The Code says:—

"For abandoning a wife, there must be one of the following seven grounds of divorce:

1. Sterility
2. Adultery
3. Disobedience to the father-in-law or the mother-in-law
4. Loquacity
5. Larceny
6. Jealousy
7. Bad disease

"If any of these grounds exist, the wife may be abandoned, the husband signing the necessary deed, which must be countersigned by the nearest ascendants. If any of these persons cannot write, the mark of the thumb may be made in place of the signature." The enumeration of the causes of divorce shows plainly that the *object of marriage was the perpetuation of the family cult*. The reason why sterility was made the first ground of divorce scarcely needs explanation. The commentators of the Taihō Code say that sterility here does *not* mean actual barrenness, but the *failure of male issue*. Marriage being contracted for a special object, and that object failing, it was justifiable to dissolve the union. A man was, in fact, under a moral obligation to his ancestors to do so.

Adultery is recognized by most nations as a ground of divorce; but the reasons of its recognition differ considerably in ancient and modern legislations. In the eye of the Taihō Code, it was not the immorality of the act itself, but rather the apprehended danger of the *confusion of blood*, whereby a person not in reality related to the ancestor might succeed to the worship.

The last of the grounds mentioned in the Taihō Code may be attributed to a similar cause. The hereditary nature of some diseases seems to have been early known, and the fear of the ancestors' blood becoming polluted was the chief cause of incurable diseases being recognized as a ground of divorce.

According to the new Civil Code, two kinds of divorce are recognized, *consensual* and *judicial*, the former being effected by the arrangement of the parties concerned, while the latter is awarded by the court of law on the grounds specified in Article 813 of the Code. The majority of the grounds mentioned in the Taihō Code do not find a place in the new Code, and bigamy, adultery, desertion, cruelty or gross insult, condemnation to punishments for such offences as forgery, bribery and corruption, theft, robbery, obtaining property under false pretences, embezzlement, receiving stolen goods, sexual immorality, etc., or disappearance from residence are the principal grounds of divorce there specified.

Besides the grounds above mentioned, a judicial divorce is granted in case an adopted son has married the daughter of the adopter, and the adoption is dissolved or annulled. Under such circumstances, either party is entitled to institute a suit for judicial divorce. The reason of this last rule may require a little explanation—especially as it relates to the continuation of the family cult. In the house system of the Japanese Family Law, a wife enters the house of her husband by marriage, except in the case of a *muko-yōshi*, or "adoption of son-in-law,"[1] when the husband enters the house of his wife, or in the case of marriage of an adopted son with a *kajo* (家女), or "house-daughter," or the daughter of the adopter, when no change occurs in the house relation of either spouse (Art. 788, Civil Code.). But when, in the case of a *muko-yōshi* or of the marriage of an adopted son with the "house-daughter," the adoption is either annulled or dissolved, the husband leaves the adoptive house, and returns to his original house (Art. 739.). In that case, if nothing happens, the wife

---

1. See p. 154 f.

follows her husband and enters his original house with him. The consequence of the wife's leaving her house is that the adoptive house not only loses the artificial successor, or the adopted son, but also the natural successor, that is, the "house-daughter," who may be made the "stock"—as the Japanese expression is, for she is often called "*daijo*," or "stock-daughter"—into which a scion may be grafted by adopting another man's son as her husband; so that the adoptive house is threatened with the extinction of the house, and with it, its ancestral cult. In that case, as the husband and the wife can not belong to different houses, the "house-daughter" is often confronted with a hard necessity to choose the cruel alternative of parting with her beloved husband, in order to obey the duty, which she owes to her house and her ancestors. Of course, such a thing only occurs when the "house-daughter" happens to be the sole presumptive heiress of the house. When the continuance of the family cult may be provided for in other ways, there is no necessity to have recourse to a consensual or judicial divorce, unless the husband or the wife wishes to terminate their relation notwithstanding that circumstance. As adoption and marriage make mutual conditions in the case of a *muko-yōshi* and also in the case of the marriage of an adopted son with the "house-daughter," the dissolution or annulment of one may be made the ground for asking the termination of the other, even though there may be no danger of the family cult becoming extinct by the continuance of the marriage relation.

CHAPTER VIII

Adoption

Perhaps in no department of jurisprudence is the relation between Ancestor-worship and law more clearly shown than in the law of adoption. Failing male issue, adoption was the most general method of providing for the continuity of Ancestor-worship. It was, as Fustel de Coulanges says, "a final resource to escape the much dreaded misfortune of the extinction of a worship."[1] Death without an heir to perpetuate the worship of ancestors was, as I have said, considered to be the greatest filial impiety. So, in the case of the failure of male issue, it was the duty of a house-head to acquire a son by adoption.

Many of the European legislations, which permit adoption, limit the *age of the adopter*, the majority of them, such as French, Italian,

---

1. Coulanges, *La Cité antique*, liv. II, ch. iv.

Austrian and German Codes, fixing the lowest limit of an adopter's age at fifty. The House Law of our Taihō Code provides that a person "*having no child*" may adopt one from among his *relatives within the fourth degree of kinship*, whose age does not exceed that which might have been attained by a son of the adopter's own body. According to some commentators of the Code, "having no child" here means that the adoptive father should have reached the age of *sixty* years or the adoptive mother *fifty* years, without having *male issue*. Now, in regard to limiting the age of an adopter, there is an apparent agreement between modern European legislations and our ancient Code; but if we look closely into the object of that limitation, we shall find that the resemblance is only superficial. European laws permit adoption chiefly for the *consolation of a childless marriage*, and as long as there is a hope of having an issue, there is no necessity for allowing adoption. But our old Code looked at the matter from another point of view. As long as there was a hope of having a male issue of blood—that is the direct descendant of his ancestor—the head of a house should not permit a person of more distant relationship to become the successor to the *sacra*. This rule took another, and apparently a contrary, form during the Shōgunate of the Tokugawa Family. In order to prevent the extinction of a house by the sudden death of a house-head, who had no son, any man over the age of *seventeen* years was allowed to adopt a son. A person between the ages of seventeen and fifty years could adopt a son even on his death-bed. Such a proceeding was called " matsugo-yōshi " (末期養子), or " adoption at the last moment " or " death-bed adoption "; or " kyū-yōshi " (急養子), or " quick adoption "; or sometimes, " niwaka-yōshi " (遽養子), or " sudden adoption." But if he failed in his duty of providing for the continuity of his house until after he had attained the age of fifty, he was threatened with a dire consequence of the extinction of his house in the event of his dying without male issue, for, the "death-bed adoption" was not permissible after the age of fifty. If he did not provide for the succession to the ancestors' *sacra* early in life, even if he still had the hope of having a male issue, he incurred the risk of the extinction of his house and the forfeiture of his feudal estate. The prohibition of the "death-bed adoption" is not in force to-day, and has not, therefore, been incorporated in the new Code. On the contrary, Article 848 of the Civil Code permits a person to make an adoption even by testament. The old and the new laws seem on this point to contradict each other, but the spirit of both is the same. They both had the perpetuation of the house for their object and the difference between them consists in this :—the one wished to make people provide for the succession early in life, by attaching severe penalties to the neglect of that precaution, while the other desires, by freely countenancing adoption, to avoid the chance of a house-worship becoming extinct.

With regard to the *lower limit of the age of the adopter*, both the laws of the Tokugawa Shōgunate and our new Civil Code agree in giving the widest scope to adoption. The Taihō Code fixed the limit at *sixty*, as I have said, but the laws of the Tokugawa Shōguns allowed and encouraged any childless head of a house over the age of *seventeen*, and even, by special permission, a person under that age, to adopt a successor; and Article 837 of the new Civil Code allows any person who has attained his *majority* to adopt another person. European laws allow adoption only in old age, because it is intended for the consolation of childless marriage, while Japanese law countenances adoption by young people, in order that the possibility of family-cult becoming extinct may be obviated.

As to the *difference of ages* which must exist between the adopter and the adopted, many European legislations, following the rule of the Roman law " adoptio naturam imitatur," require that the adopter should be older than the adopted at least by the age of puberty. For instance, German, Austrian and Italian laws require that there should be at least a difference of *eighteen* years, and the French Civil Code requires a difference of *fifteen* years between them. But in this respect, Japanese law does not strictly follow the principle of the imitation of nature, in order to give wider freedom to adoption and greater security for the continuance of worship. The Taihō Code required that the adopter and the adopted should be " fit to be father and son " (於昭穆合者); and the commentators of the Code say, that as a person over fifteen years of age was qualified to marry in accordance with that Code, " fit to be father and son " means that there should exist at least a difference of *fifteen* years. But this rule was not followed in later days. In the time of the Tokugawa Shōgunate, the adopter was only required to be older than the adopted; but frequent deviations were made from this rule by special permission—notably, a decree allowing a house-head under seventeen years of age to make an adoption, and another by which even an older person might be adopted as a son. Article 838 of the new Civil Code provides that a person cannot adopt one older than himself, although he may adopt any person who is younger than himself.

As to the *age of the adopted*, no limit has been fixed in our law. Even a baby can be adopted, and it even frequently happens that two families agree to adopt an expected child as soon as it is born. Article 843 of the Civil Code runs as follows:—"If the person to be adopted is under fifteen years of age, the parents in the same house may consent to the adoption on his or her behalf." In this respect again, there is a difference between our law and that of European countries, for, according to the latter, a person under the age of consent cannot be adopted as a general rule.

That the object of adoption was the perpetuation of Ancestor-worship may also be inferred from the old strict rule that *only a kinsman could be adopted as a son* (異姓不養). The Taihō Code limited it to within the kindred of the *fourth degree*. From the remains of the Taihō Criminal Code (戶婚律), which have come down to us, we know that a penalty of one year's penal servitude was inflicted upon any one who adopted a son from a different clan, and one of fifty floggings upon anybody who assisted him. This prohibition against the adoption of a person not related in blood, seems to have been observed till the time of the Tokugawa Shōgunate. It derives its origin from a belief mentioned in the "Commentaries of Sa on the Spring and Autumn History of Confucius" (春秋左氏傳) that "Spirits do not accept sacrifices from strangers; people do not offer sacrifices to strangers' spirits." (神不歆非類, 民不祀非族) There is a law enacted in the beginning of the Tokugawa Shōgunate, that is, the first year of Genna (元和, 1615 A. D.), that adoption must be made from persons of the same clan-name, that is, from the descendants of the ancestor of the adopter. This rule, as well as the prohibition of "death-bed adoption" before mentioned, was so strictly enforced that many feudal lords' houses became extinct on account of the failure of heirs; and in consequence, their estates were forfeited, and thousands of their vassals, or *samurai*, lost their feudal stipend. The result was that those *rōnin*, or members of the military class who had lost their feudal stipend, and could not, and would not if they could, earn a living by agriculture or commerce, became seditionaries. They often incited insurrections and joined in civil commotions, which were very frequent in the beginning of the Tokugawa Shōgunate. The government soon saw that the relaxation of this strict law of adoption was necessary in order to maintain peace in the country. In the fourth year of Keian (慶安, 1651 A. D.), immediately after the famous plot of Yui-no Shōsetsu (由井正雪) to overthrow the Tokugawa Shōgunate, an important modification was introduced into the law of adoption. From that time, adoption from different clans was not strictly forbidden, but the amended law enjoined that a man, who had no son, should adopt one from the same clan, although in case of failure of a suitable person, permission might be obtained to adopt a person of a different clan. At the same time a proviso was introduced into the law, prohibiting "death-bed adoption," that if a man having no son should be under fifty years of age, and, at his last moment, should make an application to adopt a son, the validity of such application should be determined according to the circumstance of each case. Although these laws of adoption were revised and amended several times, this rule remained substantially the same for more than two hundred years, till the end of the Tokugawa Shōgunate. The rigorous rule of prohibiting "death-bed adoption" and of limiting adoption to persons of the same clan-name practically lost its force by the introduction of the just-mentioned proviso, and it has not, therefore, been adopted in the new Code.

Another requirement of adoption, which is found in the laws of many countries, is the absolute *failure of male issue*. The House-law of the Taihō Code only allowed adoption, provided that a man had no son. This rule has been uniformly observed from ancient times down to the present day, and the new Civil Code also retains that rule, with, however, certain modifications. Article 839 provides that "a person having a male child who is the legal presumptive heir to the headship of a house is not allowed to adopt a son. But this rule does not apply to the case of adopting a son for the purpose of making him the husband of a daughter of the adopter." The object of this rule is clear from what has been pointed out before. There is no necessity for adopting a stranger, when there is a son to succeed to the house-headship.

There is one form of adoption called *muko-yōshi* (婿養子), or "adoption of son-in-law."

As has already been stated, the law considered a man childless, even though he had a daughter. Males were the only continuators of worship. Our common form of expression in offering congratulations upon the birth of another person's male child is " Kotoni go-nanshi de o-medetō ! " " I congratulate you the more, as the child is a son." A mother who has given birth to a son is praised by her relatives and friends for her " meritorious deed " (*tegara*), in having brought forth a successor to the house; for formerly it was a strict rule that only males could become house-heads and perpetuators of the cult. Those who had daughters only were, therefore, obliged to adopt a son; but it was necessary for the blood of the ancestor to be, if possible, *continued in the house*. In such cases, a house-head selects a person as his adopted son, who is fit to be his daughter's husband. If adoption and marriage take place *at the same time*, it is called *muko-yōshi*. This form of adoption is very common, and is recognized by the new Civil Code (Art. 839,

Civil Code, and Art. 100 of the Law of Registration).

But the marriage of the adopted son and the daughter of the adoptive father, or the "house-daughter," may take place subsequently to the act of adoption, for, although Article 769 of the Civil Code prohibits marriage between collateral blood relations within the third degree of kinship, collateral relationship of brothers and sisters *by adoption* is no bar to their marriage. A person who has a daughter frequently adopts a son with the expectation that the adopted son should marry his daughter when they grow up, and in most cases the parents' wishes are fulfilled. In cases where the parties do not wish to marry, dissolution of adoption very often takes place, either, because the adopted son thinks it his duty to leave the house, so that the daughter may remain in it and marry a second adopted son, thus preserving the blood of the ancestor in the house; or, because the adoptive father desires the dissolution from the same motive.

ADOPTION

The rules as to the necessity of obtaining the consent of the house-head and parents, and the consequences of the violation of those rules being nearly the same as those in the case of marriage, I do not consider it necessary to repeat them here (Arts. 750, 845, 857, Civil Code).

The effect of adoption is that the adopted son acquires the same position as a natural-born legitimate child (Art. 860, Civil Code). He relinquishes the original house and its cult, and enters into the house of the adopter, taking the house-name and clan-name of the latter (Arts. 860, 861, Civil Code). The consequence of his acquiring the status of an actual son and entering the house of the adoptive parent is, that he becomes the legal presumptive heir to the headship of the house, and, thereby, the continuator of the house-cult, or, as the Romans expressed it, " He renounced the worship of the paternal family (amissis sacris paternis)[1], and passed to that of the adoptive family (in

---

1. Cicero, *Pro Domo*, 13.

sacra transiit)."[1]

From what I have stated, it may, I think, be laid down as a general rule that *adoption had its origin in Ancestor-worship*; and the stronger the belief in that practice among the people, the wider is the scope allowed for adoption by the law.

---

1. Valerius Maximus, VII, 7.

CHAPTER IX

THE DISSOLUTION OF ADOPTION

The law relating to the dissolution of adoption also shows a close connection between the institution of adoption and Ancestor-worship. Two kinds of dissolution are recognized by the Civil Code: *dissolution by consent* and *dissolution by judicial decree*.

Adoption may be dissolved for any cause, provided that the parties mutually agree; but for its compulsory dissolution an action must be brought by one of the parties on the basis of one of the grounds specified in Article 866 of the Civil Code. I will only mention two grounds for dissolution, which have a direct bearing on Ancestor-worship. One of them is that " if the adopted person commits a grave fault of a nature to *disgrace the family-name* or ruin the " house-property " *of the adoptive house*, the adoptive parent may bring an action for the dissolution of the adoptive tie; the reason for this rule being, that the name of the ancestor's house is sacred, and it is not only his legal right, but his moral and religious duty, to dissolve the tie. The adoptive house is not the house of the adopter alone, nor is it the house of the adopted, but it is the house, which the adopter *inherited from his ancestor and will leave to his descendants*. It is the duty of every househead to preserve it, and leave it, unblemished.

Another ground for dissolution mentioned in the Code has reference to *muko-yōshi*, or the "adoption of son-in-law," and to the case of the marriage of an adopted son with "*kajo*" or the "house-daughter." If the adopted son marries the daughter of the adopter, and afterward divorce or the annulment of that marriage takes place, an action for the dissolution of adoption may be brought by one of the parties (Art. 866, Civil Code). The reason of this last rule has been already explained. If the adopted son-in-law, who is in most cases the legal presumptive heir, remains in the adoptive house and perhaps takes a second wife from another family, the true blood of the ancestor will not be continued in the house. Moreover, if the adopted son remained in the adoptive house, he would usually be obliged to live in the same house with his divorced wife—a condition of life which will be most disagreeable and often unbearable, especially when he takes a second wife. Sometimes, however, by the arrangement of the parties concerned, the adopted son-in-law remains in the adoptive house after the divorce of the "house-daughter," and even marries another person—especially when divorce took place on account of the fault of the "house-daughter." But in such cases, the divorced wife usually lives apart from the adopted son, or is given in marriage to another family. It is almost needless to say that these are exceptional cases occasioned by particular circumstances. The "adoption of son-in-law," and the marriage of an adopted son with the "house-daughter" were, as I have said before, customs based on the desire to retain the true blood of the ancestor in the family; and if the marriage is dissolved or annulled, the intention of the adopter is thereby thwarted. This rule corresponds to that relating to the dissolution of marriage which allows judicial divorce, when, in the case of "adoption of son-in-law," or in a case where the adopted son is married to the "house-daughter," the dissolution of adoption takes place.

CHAPTER X

SUCCESSION

The law of succession seems to have passed through *three stages of evolution* : first, the *succession of sacra* ; second, the *succession of status* ; and third, the *succession of property*. Each stage of development, however, did not form a distinct period in itself, but the later was gradually evolved out of the earlier by the process of differentiation. In ancient times, the duty of performing and continuing the *worship* rested on the head of the house. The house-head, as continuator of the ancestral *sacra*, was, in one sense, the representative of the ancestors. He exercised *authority* over the members of his house, because he was the representative of their ancestors. He owned the *house-property*, because it had been left by the ancestors. As the power of the house-head over house-members and house-property was the power of his ancestors, and as the continuator of the worship represented his ancestors, whoever succeeded to the house-worship succeeded to the house-headship. In those times, therefore, *the continuation of the house-cult formed the sole object of inheritance.* As a well-known maxim in the Roman Pontifical Law has it, "Nulla hereditas sine sacris," there was no inheritance without worship.

The Taihō Code (701 A. D.) represents the first stage of succession law above mentioned.

In the Succession Law, or "Keishi-ryō" (禮嗣令), of that Code, there is a provision that if a presumptive heir of a noble family is not fit to succeed to the "*important duty*" (不任承重) owing to the committal of crime or to disease, he may be disinherited and another presumptive heir may be substituted. The official commentary on this Code "Ryō-no-gigé" (令義解) says, "*to succeed to the important duty*" means "to succeed a father and *inherit the sacra*, for the matter of worship is the most important." It appears from this rule that, at that time, the continuation of Ancestor-worship was the principal object of succession.

But with the development of the house-system, the authority of the house-head, which comprehended both power over house-members and rights over house-property, came to be considered by itself as the object of inheritance. Already, in the latter half of the twelfth century of the Christian era, or probably earlier, the word *katoku* (家督) which literally means *house-authority*, was frequently used not only in its proper and original meaning, but also as the *object of inheritance* or as *successor to house-headship*. These derivative uses of the word *katoku* frequently occur in the Azuma Kagami (吾妻鏡), which is the diary of the Kamakura Shōgunate from 1180 to 1266 A. D. The use of the word *katoku as the eldest son* occurs in an old Chinese history (家有長子曰 家督—史記, 越世家) and its corresponding use in our country may have probably been derived from it. The word *katoku-sōzoku* (家督相續), or " succession to house-authority," has also been used to designate *succession to house-headship*, and this expression is still retained in the new Civil Code. Thus, in the second stage, succession represented the continuity of the *status of house-headship*, and the continuity of house-headship implied the continuity of house-worship.

The authority of the house-head included, as I have said above, both power over persons and power over property. Of these two constituent elements of the house-head's authority, the former was considered to be of far greater importance at first; but as time went on, and as the house-system was definitely settled, the latter gradually grew in importance, until finally it came to be regarded as of equal, if not of greater, importance. With the development of the economical condition of the people, importance was attached more and more to the property side of the house-head's authority, as it became clear that the continuity of the house and its cult depended upon the preservation of house-property. Then, another change in the meaning

of the word *katoku* set in. It was used to designate *house-property*, especially *house-property regarded as the object of inheritance*, just as the word " familia " in the Roman Law was used to designate not only members of the Roman family, that is, a group of persons subject to the same paterfamilias, but also the *family estate*. It is interesting to note, by the way, that the earliest use of the word " familia " in this sense occurs in the Twelve Tables in relation to succession :—
" *agnatus proximus familiam habeto.*"

In order to guard against a hasty conclusion, I must state at once that this transition in the meaning of the word *katoku* does not imply a corresponding change in the nature of succession to house-headship. It does not imply that succession to house-headship has, from being succession to status, become succession to property. It indicates, on the contrary, that there has been a corresponding change in the constituent elements of the status of house-headship. The status of house-headship included, at first, private, as well as public, rights and duties. It included not only the power over house-members and house-property, but also the capacity to fill public positions, liability to pay taxes and render public services, etc.—rights which were denied to, and duties which were not imposed upon, house-members. But after the Restoration, house-headship lost much of its public character, and the capacity to hold public offices, the liability to pay taxes and the like, ceased to be the exclusive rights and duties of the house-head. What remains now of house-headship consists chiefly of rights and duties of a private nature, and are regulated by the Civil Code. The two constituent elements of house-headship at present are authority over house-members and rights over house-property. The change in the meaning of the word *katoku* above mentioned, shows that the *former, or the personal element* of house-headship predominated at first; but with the progress of the economical condition of the people, the *latter, or the material element* began to grow in importance, until, at last, it was often spoken of as if it constituted the sole object of inheritance. Nevertheless, *katoku-sōzoku* has always been, and still is, *succession to status*, and house-property only passes to the heir as an appendage to the status of the house-head. Throughout all these changes in the constituent elements of house-headship, succession to house-headship has always retained the character of its being succession to house-worship. As it was in Greece and Rome, so in Japan a property could not be acquired without the worship, or the worship without the property. As Cicero says: "Religion prescribes that the property and the worship of a family shall be inseparable, and that the care of the sacrifices shall always devolve upon the one who receives the inheritance."[1]

There are many rules still remaining, which show that the foundation of succession to house-headship is the necessity of continuing the wor-

---

1. Cicero, *De Legibus*, II, 19, 20.

ship of ancestors. Among them, I may mention Article 987 of the Civil Code, which contains the following provision :—

"The ownership of the genealogical records of the house, of the utensils of house-worship, and of the family tombs, belongs to the special rights of succession to the headship of a house."

This important provision means that those things which are specified therein form the special objects of inheritance. They cannot be bequeathed away, nor can they be seized for debt.

Property succession, therefore, did not supersede status succession or succession to the family-cult, but grew up *by their side* in the manner I am going to describe below.

With the gradual disintegration of the house-system, and the consequent growth of individualism, the notion of individual property began to arise besides corporate property. In Japan, this stage was reached after the Restoration of 1868. Under the old regime, a house was, in the strict sense, a corporation, and the house-member could not have separate property of his own. All he gained, he gained for the house-head, or rather the house; all he possessed or enjoyed, he possessed or enjoyed by the license of the house-head, not as of right. No question of succession to the property of house-members could, therefore, arise at that time. But the Restoration completely changed this state of things. Formerly, public offices were, in most cases, hereditary, and it was only house-heads that could hold them. But it was one of the policies of the new Imperial Government to appoint its officials not, as before, on account of birth, but on account of personal merit, no distinction whatever being made as to whether they were house-heads or house-members. During the first years of the Imperial Government, statesmen and soldiers who had served in the cause of the Restoration were rewarded with pensions in life or perpetual annuities. But many of the receivers of pensions were house-members, who were otherwise not entitled to hold any property of their own. Now, these pensions and the salaries of civil and military officials of the new Government, having been given by the State for personal services, could not be treated as house-property. Thus began the independent and separate property of house-members—the first blow which the old house-system received at the hands of the Imperial Government. It is interesting to note that this is exactly what happened in the beginning of the Roman Empire, when *castrense peculium* of *filiusfamilias* was recognized for military services, and three centuries afterward *quasi-castrense peculium* for civil services.

The issue of a law in 1872, which abolished the prohibition of sale of land and granted title-deeds to landowners, the issue, in the following year, of government bonds for public loans, and the establishment of joint-stock companies and savings-banks, mark the next step in the development of the separate property of house-members. The court of law began to recognize house-members' separate property in title-deeds, bonds, stocks, debentures, savings and the like, which they held in their own names, and afterward in other things also, when their separate titles could be proved.

In this manner individual property grew up *within the house*, that is to say, a house-member began to have his own property as an individual and not as a house-member. This change took place while the house-system was still in full vigour; and the consequence was that, the devolution of this new kind of property after the death of the owner resembled more the feudal escheat than succession. It *did not descend* to the children of the deceased, but *ascended to the house-head*. But this was only a transitional phenomenon. The new Civil Code has corrected this unnatural state of things. It gives the right of succession to the *nearest descendants equally*, whether they are males or females, or whether they are in the same house with the deceased or not, the right of representation being always given to the children of a pre-deceased descendant. After the descendant comes the surviving consort; next in order, the lineal ascendant; and as the *last successor*, the *house-head* (Arts. 992–996). The new Civil Code thus recognizes *two kinds of succession*: succession to *house-headship*, or *katoku-sōzoku*; and *succession to property*, or *isan sōzoku* (遺產相續)—succession to *status* and succession to *property* existing side by side.

Four kinds of heirs to house-headship are recognized by the new Civil Code: the "*legal heir*," the "*appointed heir*," the "*chosen heir*," and the "*ascendant heir*." The legal heir, who comes first in the order of succession, is the lineal descendant of a house-head, who *is at the same time a member of his house*. Among lineal descendants, the nearest kinsman is preferred to the remote, the male to the female, and the legitimate child to the illegitimate, seniors in age being always accorded priority when they are equal in other respects (Art. 970, Civil Code). Modern writers on law usually give as a reason for the preference of nearer to remoter kinsmen, that the order of succession is determined by the *degree of affection*, which the deceased is presumed to have entertained towards his relatives, and also by the presumed intention of the person, who dies intestate as to the disposition of his property. For the preference of males to females, *feudal reasons* are often given. These reasons also form the principal basis of our present law. But here, again, the reasons for the *existence* of the rule and its *origin* are not the same. Originally, the *nearest in blood to the ancestors worshipped*, and their male descendants were preferred, because they were considered to be the fittest persons to offer sacrifices to the spirits of ancestors.

The legal heir is *heres necessarius* and is not *allowed to renounce* succession, whilst other kinds of heirs are at liberty to accept or renounce the inheritance, or to accept it with the reservation, that they shall not be liable for the debts of their predecessors. It is the bounden duty of a descendant, who is the legal heir, to accept the inheritance and continue the sacra of the house.

The house-head, on the other hand, cannot bequeath away from him more than one half of the property (Art. 1130, Civil Code), nor can he disinherit him, unless there exists one of the grounds mentioned in Article 975 of the Civil Code. The causes especially mentioned there are: (1) ill-treatment or gross insult to the house-head; (2) unfitness for house-headship on account of bodily or mental infirmities; (3) sentence to punishment for an offence of such a nature as to defile *the name of the house*; and (4) interdiction as a spendthrift. For these and any other just causes, a house-head may, with the consent of the family council, bring an action against his legal presumptive heir with a view to depriving him of the right of succession. All of the grounds mentioned in the Code relate directly or indirectly to Ancestor-worship and the necessity of maintaining intact the reputation and property of the house.

In case there is no legal presumptive heir to a house-head, the latter may *appoint* an heir, either in his lifetime or by his will. But this appointment ceases to be valid, when he obtains a child in the course of nature or by adoption, for the latter will become his legal presumptive heir (Art. 979, Civil Code).

If, at the time of the death of a house-head, there is neither a legal heir nor an appointed heir, the father of the deceased, or, if there is no father, or, if he is unable to express his intention, the mother, or, if there are no parents or both are unable to express their intention, the family council, *chooses* an heir from among the members of the house according to the following order: (1) the surviving wife, if she is a *house-daughter*; (2) the brothers; (3) the sisters; (4) the surviving wife, who *is not a house-daughter*; and finally (5) the lineal descendants of brothers and sisters (Art. 982, Civil Code).

Now, in this also, the desire for preserving the blood of ancestors will be seen from the order in which the heir is chosen. The surviving consort of the last house-head comes *first* in the order of succession, provided that she is a *house-daughter*, but comes *fourth* if she is not a descendant in blood of an ancestor of the house.

If there is neither a legal, nor an appointed, nor a chosen, heir, then *the nearest lineal ascendant* of the last house-head succeeds, the male being always preferred to the female in the case of persons standing in the same degree of relationship (Art. 984, Civil Code).

If there are no heirs such as above mentioned, the family council must choose one from among other relatives of the last house-head or the members of his house, the heads of branch-houses or the members of the principal house or branch-houses. If none of the persons above mentioned be existing, or able to succeed, then, as the last resort, the family council must choose the heir from among other persons (Art. 985, Civil Code).

From the foregoing enumeration of the various kinds of heirs, it will be seen that the law takes every precaution against the contingency of a house becoming extinct; for, with the extinction of the house, the worship of its ancestors would come to an end.

Appendix I.

A letter to the author from the late Prof. John Westlake, the noted English jurist and expert in international law:—

6 May 1902   The River House,
Chelsea Embankment,
London, S. W.

Dear Sir,

Mr. Fukai, whom I have had the great pleasure of seeing here, has given me, as from you, a copy of your work on ancestor-worship and Japanese law. I thank you much for it, and have read it with deep interest. To find ancestor-worship living among a people who can describe it from all the points of view of Europeans, is what fifty years ago would have been thought impossible. I agree with you that love must have *predominated over* fear in the feelings entertained towards ancestors, *as soon as the conviction that they still lived was reached.* But how was that conviction reached? If dreams and strange appearances of the night implanted the conviction, must not the weird horror which is apt to seize on us at night have contributed *some*, though perhaps a slight, element of dread, and therefore some element of propitiation into the worship? But this is only a suggestion with which you will be better able to deal than I.

> Believe me to be yours very truly
> J. Westlake

Mr. Nobushige Hozumi

Appendix II.

A review of the "Ancestor-worship and Japanese Law" and "Lectures on the Japanese Civil Code as material for the study of comparative jurisprudence," which appeared in the January number of the Law Quarterly Review for 1914:—

The first named of these works (sc. "Ancestor-worship and Japanese Law") is an expanded version of an essay noticed here some years ago. Although the learned author has carefully avoided controversial expressions, and has not said a word against any religion or ritual used among other nations, he has received some gratuitous and, it would seem, exceedingly foolish criticism from sundry missionaries—who perhaps do not know that there are different degrees of worship, or understand that the family *sacra* of Japan and China are compatible with several distinct forms of Asiatic religion (not to speak of a reconciliation with Christianity which at one time seemed quite possible in China). It is interesting to learn from a Japanese scholar who has no mean knowledge of Western legal history to what extent ancestor-worship has influenced Japanese institutions. Its marks are most obvious, as might be expected, in the law of succession and adoption. Thus adoption outside the clan was formerly not allowed, for 'spirits do not accept sacrifices from strangers' (contrast with this the early Roman law which held it better that the *sacra* should be performed even by a mere trespasser than not at all).

The lectures on the Civil Code are chiefly concerned with 'those parts in which the indigenous element is usually most persistent,' namely personal and family law, and therefore some of the information given in the essay on ancestor-worship is duplicated. In some cases where archaic institutions are still recognized by law, such as abdication of family headship for the purpose of becoming a hermit or devotee, one would like to know how far they are maintained in modern practice. The learned author calls attention to the great improvement effected in the position of women under the modern system, and to other reforms. He points out that the Japanese Code is not (as at one time it seemed likely to be) imitated from any one European system, but has been framed after careful comparison of many codes and systems, though, in the form it finally assumed, the terminology and arrangement are more German than anything else. It is interesting to know that a new Japanese word had to be coined to express 'right' in the sense of a legal claim or title. The English word, of course, is not free from ambiguity, neither are the words covering the field of 'law' and 'right' in other European tongues. 'Gesetz' is less vague than 'law,' but 'Recht' is much vaguer than 'right.' Again, we are familiar with some pretty troublesome puzzles in translating Roman law terms. Prof. Hozumi's historical comments, which we hope he will expand some day, are judicious and, so far a Western lawyer's imperfect knowledge can follow him, correct.

Editor's Note

This is a new edition of a book by my father, the late Prof. N. Hozumi. He was born in 1855, and, since 1871, studied law in Tokyo as one of the first regular students of Western legal science in Japan. Going to London in 1876 to prosecute his study, he entered the Middle Temple and studied the English jurisprudence at the height of the Victorian age. Besides, during his sojourn there he came to be greatly influenced by the theories of evolution of Darwin and Herbert Spencer—an influence which fully developed itself, many years afterwards, in his "Treatise on the Evolution of Law," a major work in my father's later life. Called to the Bar in 1879, he proceeded to Berlin to make a study of Roman law and German and French laws at the University there. On his return home in 1881, he was made a lecturer in the Faculty of Law of the Tokyo Imperial University, and was raised to a professor in the following year. For thirty years since then, that is, from 1881 to 1912, he lectured, in the main, on the private law and the philosophy of law. My father received the doctorate of Hōgaku-hakushi early in his academic career, and was awarded the title of Honorary Professor when he finally left the University. Previously to this, he had the membership of the Imperial Academy, and later on, appointed President of that body, he made his utmost efforts for the promotion of international intellectual co-operation as well as for the advancement of national scientic research. Moreover, taking part in legislative work, my father collaborated with other jurists to draft and compile the Civil Code and various other legal codes of this country. For the services he thus rendered to the State he was created Baron in 1915, and was designated Privy Councillor, subsequently being raised to Vice-President, and then to President. He died of illness in 1926, at the age of seventy-one.

In addition to his five years' stay abroad for study, my father visited Europe and America twice in his later life. In October 1899 he attended, as the Japanese delegate, the International Congress of Orientalists held at Rome, and again, in September 1904 he was present, in the same capacity, at the International Congress of Arts and Sciences at Saint Louis, U. S. A.

His lectures delivered on these two occasions were afterwards published in book-form. The lecture given at Saint Louis is, in substance, the same as his book "The New Japanese Civil Code as material for the study of comparative jurisprudence," and the one delivered at Rome makes the essential part of the present work on Japanese ancestor-worship.

"Ancestor-worship and Japanese Law" first appeared in 1901, as a booklet of seventy-five pages. That it attracted the attention of Occidental scholars is shown, for instance, by a letter from the late Prof. John Westlake printed at the end of the present edition (Appendix I). After ten years the second edition came out, enlarged to a volume of nearly 200 pages. In the author's own words, he has "thoroughly revised the original lecture, reconsidered and rewritten it, and made considerable additions to it," so that the new issue could scarcely be called a second edition. From the Preface to the second edition, again, from which the foregoing is quoted, the author's motive for bringing out a new edition may easily be gathered. While his book met with favourable reception by scholars both at home and abroad—so much so that it was quoted, amongst others, by Giddings in his "Descriptive and Historical Sociology" (1906)—it received adverse criticism from some Christian missionaries. His wish to dispel the misunderstandings on the part of the religious circles on the one hand and to expand and amplify his theory in behalf of his fellow scientists on the other hand, most probably led him to take up his pen for revision and rewriting. His Preface above referred to is in itself a short treatise which may well bear the title "Compatibility of the Practice of Ancestor-worship with Christianity." The truth of that compatibility, I believe, however, has been fully admitted in the intervening years, so that my father's explanation and elucidation would hardly be necessary to-day. In bringing about this state of things, it may be said, the present book has given its small share side by side with the works of such writers as Lafcadio Hearn, Prof. Y. Haga, and Prof. J. Takakusu—writers who are quoted elsewhere in these pages. In 1913 the third revised edition was published. Both the second and the third editions won a favourable reception from the learned circles in Europe and America, and were reviewed in various foreign journals for jurisprudence or sociology. In Appendix II of the present edition is reprinted an article which appeared in "The Law Quarterly Review" (January 1914) treating of "Ancestor-worship" jointly with the same author's "The New Japanese Civil Code." It will be of some interest to compare it with my father's argument in his Preface to the second edition.

It is a quarter of a century since the publication of the third edition, and thirteen years since the author's death. In the present day, when there is, among our people, a loud cry for the fresh recognition of the Japanese spirit, and in foreign countries, an eager desire for a real knowledge of Japan and things Japanese, there seems to be a growing demand for a perusal of my father's book on account of its subject-matter. I have ever thought it a pity that the copies in stock were not enough to meet this demand. It is a great pleasure to me, therefore, that the publication of the fourth edition will remove this difficulty. After the third edition had come out, the author was collecting new material in preparation for future editions, so that if he were living now, the present edition must have appeared with further revisions and in a much enlarged form. As a memorial of the author who is no more, however, I thought it advisable to reprint the contents of the last edition with a minimum of alterations, except for corrections of typographical errors. But three photographs have been added, of which one, given as the frontispiece, is a portrait of the author about the time of his lecture at Rome, and the other two are of the sacrifices offered before his coffin and before his tomb. The photographs of the Japanese Shintō worship in the third edition show the ceremonies performed for the soul of Prof. Yatsuka Hozumi, the author's younger brother who died earlier than he. We had the least idea at the time that photographs of the author's own funeral would be inserted in the next edition.

The publication of the present edition, like that of the second edition, has been made possible by the financial support of the Hozumi Foundation for the Encouragement of Legal Science. In his Preface to the second edition the author said, "I take this as a proper opportunity to acknowledge publicly my deep sense of gratitude towards the subscribers to the endowment of that Foundation, who numbered more than one thousand, for their kindness in thus memorializing my small share in the legal education of this country. I have also to return my hearty thanks to the directors of the Foundation, Professors Keijirō Okano, Saburō Yamada and Kōtarō Shida for proposing to appropriate the income of the Foundation, in the first place, to the publication of my book, and to the members of the Council for unanimously resolving to adopt the proposal and make it the first act of the Foundation." I, as son and successor to the author, repeat these words here, with necessary alterations, with a still greater sense of gratitude towards the subscribers and officers of the Foundation. Of the three professors named above, Prof. Okano passed away before my father, but Profs. Yamada and Shida are still on the Council, and along with the rest of the original members and the newly-appointed ones, superintend the affairs of that body with constant care and unflagging zeal. It was solely due to the support of the Foundation that after his death my father's works were brought out in quick succession. The publication of the second edition of this book was, as quoted above, the first undertaking of the Foundation, and this, I believe, adds a great deal to the significance of the assistance it has rendered to the appearance of the present edition. It is also my pleasant duty to express my best thanks to Prof. Sanki Ichikawa of the

Tokyo Imperial University and Mr. Tatsu Sasaki, a lecturer at the same University. Prof. Ichikawa, reading through the last edition on its appearance, kindly pointed out, to the author who was yet alive, the misprints and inaccuracies in wording and expression, which have been duly corrected in the present issue. Mr. Sasaki read the proof-sheets with close care, and otherwise saw the book through to its completion.

The most everyday form of ancestor-worship in a Japanese home, as is stated in the book, is to offer, on the family-altar, the flower or food which the dead ancestors most loved. My father's favourite flower was the rose, and his favourite food grilled sardine à la Japonaise. So in my household we never omit to offer this flower and this dish to his spirit from time to time, on due occasions. It is, indeed, in great joy and sincere gratitude that I say I am now able to make an offering to my dead father which will please him far better than the flower or the fish.

Shigetō Hozumi,
Son and successor to the original author.

Tokyo,
August, 1938.

INDEX

A

Abolition of a house, 116, 117.
Accession of Jimmu Tennō, 39, 84.
Accession of the Emperor, 84, 85, 96, 97, 98.
Adopted son, 128, 140–143, 148–150, 154–157, 160–162.
Adopter, 144–150, 155, 157, 159, 160, 162.
Adoption, 118, 131, 141–143, 144–158, 159–162, 177.
Adoption of son-in-law, 131, 141, 154, 160–162.
Adoptive father, 145, 156, 159.
Adultery, 138, 139, 140.
Agamaena, 48.
Age of the adopted, 150.
Age of the adopter, 144, 145, 150.
Aged, treatment of the, 8–12.
Ama-no-Koyane-no Mikoto, 49.
Amaterasu Ō-Mikami, 30, 33, 85.
"Analects of Confucius," 15.
Ancestor, 8, 9, 20–25, 54, 142, 143, 155, 156, 161, 163, 164, 177.
Ancestor-worship, 1, 2, 4, 7, 9, 14, 16, 19, 23–25, 30–32, 33, 44, 45, 54, 55, 71, 86–88, 102, 103, 106, 117, 118, 121, 122, 133, 135, 137, 142, 144, 151, 158, 159, 163, 164, 165, 169, 170, 176.
Ancient code, 145.
Anniversary of ancestors, 16, 45, 55.
Annual Festival, 44.
Annulment of marriage, 127.
Appointed heir, 174, 177.
"Aryan Household," 106.
Ascendant heir, 174, 178.
Austrian Code, 145.
Austrian Law, 149.
Autumnal Sacrifice, 40.
Avatars of Buddha, 88.
Avebury, Lord, 3, 7.
"Azuma Kagami," 165.

B

Bad disease, 138, 140.
Ban-betsu, 47.
Battle of Awazu, 59.
Battle of the Japan Sea, 73, 83.
Battle of the Uji River, 59.
Bigamy, 140.
Birth in the Imperial Family, 93.

INDEX

Bon Festival, 65.
Bon-ichi, 65.
"Book of Filial Piety," 125.
"Book of House Ceremonies," 12.
"Book of Rituals," 124.
Branch-house, 116, 117, 178.
Brother, 177.
Buddhism, 2, 29, 88.
"Buddhist altar," 30.
Buddhist rituals, 63, 66.
Buddhists, 3, 31, 55, 88.
Bureau of Genealogical Investigation, 112.
Butsudan, 30–32, 68.

C

Castrense peculium, 172.
Causes of divorce, 138-140.
Celebration Year's Festival, 42, 45.
Celibacy, 131–133.
Cenotaph, 31, 32.
Ceremony of Coronation, 96–98.
Ceremony of the Imperial marriage, 94.
Ceremony of worship, 37.
Chèng-ch'eng-kung, 102.
Chief Master of Rituals, 97.
Child, 7, 53, 129, 133, 134, 136, 145, 148, 157, 177.
Childless marriage, 148.
"Children of the clan," 53.
China, 74, 101, 102, 103.
Chinese civilization, 2, 29, 72.

Chinese history, 165.
Chinese laws, 130, 131.
Chinese philosophy, 126, 130.
Chinese revolution, 102.
Chōja, 105.
Chosen heir, 174, 177, 178.
Christianity, 88, 183, 190.
Chu-hsi, 12.
Cicero, 169.
Civil Code, Japanese, 116, 126, 129, 140, 141, 147, 148, 150, 154, 155, 156, 157, 166, 168, 170, 173, 174, 176, 177, 178, 184, 188.
Clan, 32, 47–53, 100, 104, 105, 110–113, 151–153.
Clan ancestors, 32, 47–53.
Clan-gods, 50–52.
Clan-name, 47–49, 101, 104, 110, 111, 152, 153, 157.
Clan-registry, 111–113.
Clansmen, 50.
Cleyera japonica, 30.
"Commencement of State Affairs," 71.
"Commentaries on the Constitution," 76.
Common ancestor, 23, 49, 104.
Community of blood, 49.
Compulsory dissolution of adoption, 159.
Concubinage, 133–136.
Confucianism, 2.
Confucius, 15, 125, 151.
Consanguinity, 21, 23.

INDEX

Consensual divorce, 140-143.
Consent of house-head for marriage, 127-130, 157.
Consent of parents for marriage, 127-130, 157.
Constitution, 39, 72, 75-91, 99, 107.
Constitutionalism, 86, 90-91.
Continuator of worship, 129, 135, 136, 157, 163, 164.
Continuity of the house, 116.
Continuity of worship, 118, 124, 142, 144, 163, 164.
Coronation, 84, 96-98.
Coulanges, Fustel de, 3, 15, 25, 144.
Court-officials, 50.
Criminal Codes, 136, 137.
Cruelty, 140.
Customary law, 126.

D

Dai-dai-Kagura, 35.
Daijingū, 30, 33-35, 41, 44, 72, 73, 94, 95, 97-99.
Daijo, 142.
Daijō-Sai, 84, 97.
Dajō-gwan, 72.
Darwin, Charles, 187.
Daughter, 154, 155, 156.
Daughter of the adopter, 154.
Death, 9, 10, 18, 144, 146, 147, 152, 153, 177.
"Death-bed adoption," 146, 147, 152, 153.

Death of the Emperor, 96, 97.
Death without an heir, 144.
Declaration of war, 39.
"Declaring name," 58.
Department of Divine Worship, 72, 89.
Descendants, 8, 15, 77, 78, 125, 160, 173, 177, 178.
Desertion, 140.
Development of economical condition, 166.
Disappearance from residence, 140.
Disinheritance of heir, 118, 176.
Disobedience, 138.
Dissolution by consent, 159.
Dissolution by judicial decree, 159.
Dissolution of adoption, 159-162.
"Distant worship," 41.
Divine ancestor, 85.
"Divine Branch," 47.
"Divine Mirror," 33, 85.
"Divine Sword," 85.
"Divine Treasures," 85, 97.
Divorce, 138-143.
"Doctrine of the Mean," 15.
Dread of ghosts, 7, 14, 16, 18, 24, 87, 181, 182.

E

Effect of adoption, 157.
Egoism, 9, 12.
Emperor, 37-46, 82-86, 94, 97.

98, 100, 101, 102, 103.
Empire, foundation of the, 81.
Empress, 42, 44, 45.
Eponym, 52.
European civilization, 29.
Extinction of the house, 146, 179.
Extinction of worship, 144, 147, 179.

F

Familia, 167.
Family, 3, 23, 115, 124, 127, 157, 159, 161, 162, 167.
Family council, 177, 178.
Family estate, 167.
Family-name, 124, 159.
Family system, 115.
Family worship, 54–68, 129, 133, 141, 142, 148.
"Farewell fire," 65.
Father, 177.
Female house-head, 128.
Festival, 37–45, 50, 51.
Festivals of clan-gods, 50–52.
Festival of the Emperor's Birthday, 44.
Festivals of the Prayer for the Year's Crop, 44.
Feudal estate, 147.
Filial piety, 7, 9, 11, 15, 101, 107, 126.
First Emperor, 36, 37, 39, 40, 43, 45, 75, 81, 84, 94–97, 98.
First Imperial Ancestor, 30, 32, 34, 36, 41–43, 85.
"First instalment of taxes in kind," 41.
"Five Articles of the Imperial Oath," 89.
"Five punishments," 126.
"Foreign Branch," 47.
Four kinds of heirs, 174–178.
French Code, 144, 149.
Fujiwara Clan, 50–51, 105.
Fujiwara Period, 105.
"Funa Benkei," 60–63.

G

"Gempei Seisuiki," 60.
Genealogical records, 112, 170.
Genji, 105.
Genji-no-Chōja, 105.
Genshi Sai, 38.
German Code, 145.
German Law, 149, 185.
Gesetz, 185.
Ghost, 7, 10, 14, 15, 16, 17, 18, 19, 24, 87.
Ghost of the ancestor, 15.
Ghost propitiation, 14, 19, 24, 87, 182.
Giddings, 189.
God, 40.
"God-shelf," 30, 31.
"*God's bone*," 48.
Government, 71–74, 85, 86, 89, 90, 91, 105, 106, 112, 113, 115, 152, 171, 172.
Grandparent, 126.

INDEX

Grave, 10, 41, 43, 73, 94–98.
Grave of Jimmu Tennō, 95–97.
"Great clan," 49, 105.
Great Council of State, 72.
Great Festivals, 37–43, 45.
"Great house," 100.
"Great offering," 30.
Great Shrine at Isé, 30, 33–35, 41, 44, 72, 73, 95, 97–99.
Greece, 169.
Gross insult, 140.

H

Haga, Yaichi, Dr., 100.
Hamlet, 17.
Hand-clapping, 58.
Hearn, Dr. W. E., 3, 25, 106.
Hearn, Lafcadio, 190.
Heir, 122, 174–179.
Higan, 64.
Holland, Clive, 89.
Hosokawa, Baron Junjirō, 14, 39.
House, 47, 110–123, 128, 133, 141, 142, 146, 152, 154–157, 160, 161, 170, 178, 179.
House-ancestors, 117, 120, 127.
House-authority, 165.
House-daughter, 128, 141–143, 156, 160–162, 177, 178.
House-head, 116, 117, 122, 128, 132, 144, 146, 150, 154, 155, 162, 163–171, 173–178.
House-law, 119–123.
House Law or "*Koryō*," 126, 138, 145.
House-members, 115, 116, 121–123, 163, 168–174, 178.
House-name, 157.
House-property, 115, 159, 163–169, 172, 176.
House-registry, 113–114.
House-system, 110, 165, 166, 170, 171, 173.
House-worship, 54, 116, 164, 169.
Hozumi, Yatsuka, 192.
Hozumi Foundation for the Encouragement of Legal Science, the, 192, 193.
"Hundred Articles of Tokugawa," 132.
Husband, 134, 138, 141–143, 154, 155.

I

Ihering, Rudolf von, 3, 10.
Illicium religiosum, 32.
Imperial Ancestors, 14, 30, 33–46, 73–85, 92, 92, 96, 101, 102, 107, 108, 112.
"Imperial Branch," 47.
Imperial Family, 96, 100.
Imperial heir-apparent, 94, 96, 97.
Imperial House, 37, 38, 80–82, 84, 92–103.
Imperial House Law, 80, 82, 84, 95, 98, 99.
Imperial House Ordinances, 37,

INDEX

92, 93, 96–98.
Imperial marriage, 94, 95.
Imperial message, 84.
Imperial Oath, 79–81, 89.
Imperial Palace, 43.
Imperial Rescript on Education, 46, 106–109.
Imperial Sanctuary, 44, 96.
Imperial Speech, 77.
Imperial Throne, 76, 79, 81, 82, 107.
"Important duty," 164.
Individualism, 170.
Inheritance, 169, 170, 176.
International Congress of Arts and Sciences, 188.
International Congress of Orientalists, 188.
Inkyo, 111.
Irving, Henry, 17.
Isan-sōzoku, 174.
Isé, 30, 33–36, 41, 44, 72, 73, 79.
Isé-mairi, 35.
Italian Code, 144.
Italian Law, 149.
Itō, Prince Hirobumi, 73, 75, 91.
Itō, Viscount Miyoji, 76.
Izu, 47.

J

Jealousy, 138.
Jewel, 85.
Jimmu Tennō, 36, 38–40, 43, 45, 75, 81, 84, 94–99.
Jimmu Tennō Sai, 40.
Jingi Kwan, 72.
Jones, Hartwell, 11.
Judicial divorce, 105, 140, 141, 143.

K

Kabané, 47–49.
Kabuné, 48.
Kajo, 128, 141–143, 156, 160–162, 177, 178.
Kamakura Shōgunate, 165.
Kamidana, 30, 31, 33.
Kami hone, 48.
Kan-kei-Jo, 112.
Kannamé Matsuri, 41.
Kasanui, 34.
Kashiko-Dokoro, 33–37, 41, 44, 92, 94–98.
Kashiko-Dokoro-O'kagura, 44.
Kasuga, 50.
Katoku-sōzoku, 165–169, 174.
Keian, 152.
Keishi-ryō, 164.
Kigensetsu, 39, 75, 81, 82, 98.
Kinen Sai, 44.
Kinichi, 54–56.
Kinship, 22, 106, 151, 156, 174, 175.
Kiso, Yoshinaka, 59.
Konakamura, Prof. K., 58.
Koryō, 126, 138.
Koseki, 113.
Ko-uji, 49.

INDEX

Kugadachi, 111.
Kurita, Prof., 13, 48, 58.
Kusa-ichi, 65.
Kwanpaku, 105.
Kwō-betsu, 47.
Kwōrei-Den, 36–39, 92–98.
Kyōto, 84, 97.
Kyū-yōshi, 146.

L

Lady Guardian of the Great Shrine, 35.
Larceny, 138.
Lares, 15.
Larvae, 14.
Law, 185.
Law of adoption, 144–162.
Law of registration, 110, 113, 114.
Law of succession, 163–179.
"Law Quarterly Review," 183, 190.
Lectures on National Festival Days, 14.
"Legacy of Iyeyasu," 131.
Legal heir, 160, 174.
"Li Chi," 124.
Local tutelary god, 31, 50, 52.
Loquacity, 110.
Lord Guardian of the Great Shrine, 35.
Lotus flower, 32.
Love of ghost, 19.
Lowell, Percival, 101.
Loyalty of the Japanese, 101.

M

Main house, 117, 118.
Maine, Sir Henry, 3, 25.
Majority, 122.
Majority Ceremony, 93, 95.
Male issue, 134, 139, 145–147, 154, 155.
Manchu Dynasty, 102–103.
Manes-worship, 14, 15, 24.
Marriage, 94, 118, 119, 124–137, 143, 149, 156, 156, 157, 160–162.
Master of Rituals, 37.
Matsugo-yōshi, 146.
Matsuri-goto, 71.
Mencius, 125, 129.
Mibun-tōki, 114.
Middle Ages, 88, 110.
Military conscription, 115.
Minamoto Clan, 59, 105.
Mirror, Divine, 85.
Mitama-shiro, 31.
Miya-mairi, 53.
Monogamy, 134.
Mother, 21, 177.
Mukai-bi, or "reception fire," 65.
Muko-yōshi, 141–143, 154, 155, 160–162.

N

Nai-Shinnō, 95.
Nakatomi, 49.
National holidays, 45, 98.
National morality, 100.

INDEX

National policy, 90.
National worship, 46, 99.
"Natural History of the Ten Commandments," 12.
Nenki, 54–56, 67.
New house, 116, 133.
New Year's Congratulations, 43.
New Year's Day, 35.
New Year's Festival, 43.
Nigotayé, 58.
Niinamé-Matsuri, 41.
Ninigi-no Mikoto, 33.
Niwaka-yōshi, 146.
"*Nō*," 60–63.
Norito, 57.
Nozaki-no-nusa, 41.
Nuké-mairi, 35.

O

Objects of adoption, 144, 145, 150.
Object of ancestor-worship, 12, 13.
Objects of inheritance, 165.
Occidental civilization, 87.
Offerings, 30–32, 41, 42, 50, 51, 94, 96.
Okuri-bi, or "farewell fire," 65.
Ōname-no-Matsuri, 84.
Ōnusa, 30.
Ordeal of hot water, 111.
Ordinance relating to the Ascension, 97.
Ordinance relating to the Family Relation, 92.
Ordinance relating to the Institution of the Heir-apparent, 96.
Ordinance relating to the Majority Ceremony, 93.
Ordinance relating to Regency, 98.
Oriental civilization, 87.
Origin of Ancestor-worship, 7–19.
Original house, 129, 141, 157.
Ō-uji, 49.
Ōyake, 100.

P

Parent, 7–13, 22, 126, 128, 150, 157, 177.
Peerage, 39, 119, 120.
Peerage Ordinance, 119.
People, 9, 11, 21, 23, 71, 108, 109.
Perpetuation of the house, 147.
Perpetuation of the worship, 124.
Personal registration, 110.
Political change, 1, 2.
Posthumous Buddhist name, 31.
Preamble of the Constitution, 76, 77.
Preamble of the Imperial House Law, 81, 82.
Preamble of the Supplements to the Imperial House Law, 82.
Presumptive heir, 116–118, 132, 154, 157, 160, 177.

INDEX

Primitive people, 9, 11, 21, 22.
Princes of the Blood, 39, 42, 93.
Principal house, 100, 117, 118.
Promulgation of the Constitution, 39, 72, 75, 77, 82.
Property, 115, 163–172, 176.
Property succession, 170.
Propitiation of ghosts, 7, 24, 87.
Punishments, 140.

Q

Quasi castrense peculium, 172.
"Quick adoption," 146.

R

"Reception fire," 65.
Recht, 185.
Regency, 98.
Register of clan-names, 112, 113.
Registry, 110–114.
Rei Sai, 44.
Religion, 20, 24, 25, 29, 88, 89. 109.
Restoration of 1868, the, 89, 115, 132, 168, 170, 171.
"Reverential name," 48.
Right, 185.
"Rituals of worship," 13, 38, 58, 72, 124.
Roman Law, 148, 167, 169, 184.
Romans, conception of ghosts among, 14.
Rome, 169.
Rōnin, 152.
Russo-Japanese War, 73, 83.

"Ryō-no-gigé," 164.

S

Sacra, 128–130, 146, 147, 163, 176, 184.
Sacred places in Japanese house, 30.
Sacrifice, 7, 8, 13–15.
Sacrifice day, 54, 55.
Sacrifice month, 54.
Sacrifice of the First Tribute, 41.
Sacrifice year, 54, 55.
Saga, Emperor, 112.
"*Sai-sei Itchi,*" 72.
Sai-tan Sai, 43.
Sakaki, 30, 31, 68.
Sale of land, 172.
Samurai, 133, 152.
Sanctuary of the Imperial Palace, 33, 36–38, 41, 43, 74, 82, 92.
Sansom, Mr. G. B., 61, 63.
Sasaki, Takatsuna, 59.
Seiji-Hajimé, 71.
Sen-Shizokushi-jo, 111.
Sen-Tei Sai, 42.
Seven grounds of divorce, 138.
Shihō-Hai, 43.
Shikimi tree, 32.
Shikinen Sai, 42, 45.
"Shin-betsu," 47.
Shin-Den, 36, 37, 40, 92, 94 96.
Shin-nō, 93, 95.
Shinshō Sai, 40, 41, 84.
Shintō household, 31, 32.
Shintōism, 30, 31, 87, 89.

INDEX

Shintōists, 3, 55, 56.
Shintō rituals, 56–58.
Shōgunate, 132.
"Shōjiroku," 110, 112, 113.
Shōryō-dana, 65.
Shōtsuki, 54, 56.
Shūki Kwōrei Sai, 40.
Shūki Shin-Den Sai, 40.
Shun, 129.
Shunki Kwōrei Sai, 39.
Shunki Shin-Den Sai, 40.
Sister, 177.
"Small clan," 49, 105.
Small Festivals, 37, 43–46,.
Son, 8, 132, 144, 151, 153, 154–156.
Son-in-law, 131, 141, 154, 160–162.
"Soul of the Far East," 101.
Sovereignty, 77.
Spencer, Herbert, 3, 187.
"Spirit-shelf," 66.
"Spring and Autumn History" of Confucius, 74, 151.
Spring Sacrifices, 40.
State, 76, 77, 105.
Status of house-headship, 166.
Steinmetz, Dr. S. R., 25.
Sterility, 138, 139.
"Stock-daughter," 142.
Sub-clans, 49.
Subject, 77, 78, 79, 107.
Succession, 116, 128, 130, 132, 136, 146, 147, 163–179.
Succession law, 163–179.

Succession of property, 163, 167, 170, 174.
Succession of sacra, 163, 168.
Succession of status, 163, 167, 169, 174.
Succession to house-headship, 164, 167, 173.
"Sudden adoption," 146.
Sujin, Emperor, 34.
Supplements to the Imperial House Law, 82, 99.
Sword, Divine, 85.

T

Taihō Code, 72, 126, 136, 138–140, 145, 148, 149, 151, 164.
Taikwa Era, 72, 106, 113.
Taima, 30.
Taira Clan, 61–63.
Taishō Tennō, 73.
Takakusu, Dr. J., 100, 190.
Tamagushi, 57.
Tempyō-Hōji Era, 111.
Tenchō-Setsu Sai, 44.
"Ten Treatises on the National Character," 100.
Testament, 147.
Theocratico-patriarchal constitutionalism, 86.
"Three Bodies," 104.
Three epochs of registration law, 110.
Three kinds of Ancestor-worship, 30–32.

INDEX

Three stages of succession law, 163.
Three Temples of the Imperial Sanctuary, 38, 44, 93, 94, 96, 97.
Throne, Imperial, 87, 92, 96, 97.
Tōgō, Admiral, 73, 83.
Tokugawa Shōgunate, 67, 105, 146, 148, 149–153.
Tomomori, Taira, 61–63.
Toyosukiirihime-no Mikoto, 34.
"Truant pilgrimage," 75.
Twelve Tables, 167.
Two classes of ghosts, 14.
Two kinds of divorce, 140.
Two kinds of succession, 174.
Tylor, Dr. 3, 18, 24.

U

Ubusuna-no-kami, 52.
Uchi, 47.
Uji, 47, 49, 104.
Uji-gami, 31, 50, 51, 53.
Uji-ko, 53.
Umi-chi, 47.
Unit of society, 114.
Unity of blood, 22, 23.
"Unity of worship and government." 72.
Universal institution, whether ancestor-worship is, 24, 25.
Urabon, 65.

W

Wen-t'ien-hsiang, 102.
Western civilization, 2, 87, 89.

Westlake, John, 189.
Wife, 122, 128, 133–136, 138, 141, 142, 161.
Will, 177.
Wō, 93, 95.
Worship, Ceremony of, 38.
Worship of clan-ancestors, 32, 47–53.
Worship of Imperial Ancestors, 30–32, 46, 77, 99, 104.
Worship of patron god of locality, 32.
Worship, rituals of, 72.
"Worshipping in Four Directions," 43.

X

Xavier, Francis, 88.

Y

Yamagata, Prince Aritomo, 106.
Yamato, 34, 101.
Yata-no-Kagami, 34.
"Yengi Shiki," 72.
Yōhai, 41.
Yōshi, 104, 128, 141–143, 149 155, 154–157, 160–162.
Yoshikawa, Count Akimasa, 106.
Yoshitsune, Minamoto, 61–63.
Yui-no, Shōsetsu, 152.

Z

Zushi, 32.

For Product Safety Concerns and Information please contact our EU representative GPSR@taylorandfrancis.com
Taylor & Francis Verlag GmbH, Kaufingerstraße 24, 80331 München, Germany

www.ingramcontent.com/pod-product-compliance
Lightning Source LLC
Chambersburg PA
CBHW051633230426
43669CB00013B/2291